I0011294

AFROINFORMATICS ™

Achievement is Fundamental to Responsibility and Outreach!

Dr. A. Yager Wyatt

Afroinformatics™

Copyright © 2013 by Dr. A.Yager Wyatt

All rights reserved. No part of this book may be reproduced or transmitted in any form or by any means without written permission of the author or publisher except for the use of brief quotes and citations in a review.

ISBN 978-0-692-37323-1

Library of Congress Control Number: 2015901209

Author & Editor: Dr. A. Yager Wyatt

Book Design & Artwork (as noted): Adam's ARThouse™

In Loving Memory
Of
Loretta Y. Wyatt
Mom
Educator
Cub Scout Den Mother
2.11.1935 - 2.1.2014

The Art
of

I
T

liberal arts

College or university curriculum aimed at imparting
general knowledge and developing general intellectual
capacities, in contrast to a professional, vocational, or
technical curriculum. In Classical antiquity, the term
designated the education proper to a freeman (Latin *liber*,
"free") as opposed to a slave. In the medieval Western
university, the seven liberal arts were grammar, rhetoric,
and logic (the *trivium*) and geometry, arithmetic, music,
and astronomy (the *quadrivium*). In modern colleges and
universities, the liberal arts include the study of literature,
languages, philosophy, history, mathematics, and science.

(Merriam-Webster: Concise Encyclopedia)

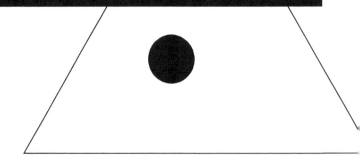

Preface

Cultural competency respecting education, health, and social development has been established as a national and global objective through government initiatives (Sellers, Smith, Shelton, Rowley, & Chavous, 1998; Varkey, 2010; Hurd et al., 2012). This has included more attention to reducing health disparities through technology. Respecting disparity reductions for minority groups or underserved populations, a responsible focus for strategic resolutions has remained.

As a community-oriented African American health professional, I have chosen this path as being personally contributory. As is common to many minority providers, I have attempted to serve our community through various means to include, private practitioner, government contractor, military officer, state employee, volunteer, mentorship and academics. The perspectives to be presented in the following chapters have been gained from those experiences. It was my aim for this reference to remain respectfully brief yet comprehensive enough to be applicable throughout the entire spectrum of academic, professional, community, and government stakeholders. As a result, aside from relevant topic quotes or narratives used to establish common cultural relationships, I chose to present the core material in a peer-reviewed format for students or educational and professional leadership to reference information in a manner to which they are accustomed. Respecting general readers, this work is my attempt at a creative expression of the material, as I have interpreted it, and reflective of my cultural experiences of 50 years to this point. However, my goal was to afford all readers with a working-knowledge to be usefully tailored for specific agendas, or towards generating dialogue for realistic solutions through evidence. To aid in initial exposures, I have provided a list of potential career alternatives at the end of their related sections. More complete explanations of those may be obtained from the Index following the main text of the book.

That being said and depending upon the level of pre-existing familiarity with informatics, the reader is advised to jump about freely for useful information related to areas of their particular concern. To put it in the words of one of our famous radio icons...*you've got deep, real deep, and not too deep!* However, it is my wish for the contents of this work to assist in the global shift towards cultural competencies respecting diversified solutions by spawning other initiatives, or serving as a possible blue-print of exposure for any ethnicity's common social uplift. Further, the chosen usages of quotes or other forms of artistic expressions were done so to respectfully promote the continued patronage, support, education, and enjoyment afforded to our communities by the original authors.

I would like to collectively commend the Hampton, Howard, and Walden University academic professors for having contributed vitally to my interpretations through a diversified intellect respecting liberal arts, professional health sciences, and informatics over the past 30 plus years. In addition, I would also like to thank all referenced contributors for their research. Originally, the book was to be edited by my mother. Unfortunately, my Virginia Union University trained *copy* critic from youth, and who would've wanted me to say that (smile), fell ill and entered eternal rest prior to its completion. However, much of its contents had already been subjected to critical review by the aforementioned professors, as it was compiled from my previously authored submissions. Thus, the work being a product of those means, I've chosen to let it stand. Plus, the alternatives just didn't feel right given the circumstances.

That being said, all appreciable technical flaws to be found by the reader are my own. Further, I wish to thank and acknowledge my father (Philip); wife (Beth) and Courtney; sister and personal *proof-reader* (Melani); Tony, Ray, and my extended family; my *Hood* fraternity of *brothers*; my HI and HU *crews*; Captain Bryant and military family, friends and colleagues for their ongoing contributions towards my personal growth. Through various means, all impacts have instilled in me a loving culture of meaningful purpose. This book is dedicated to OUR world's children; to include my offspring Billie, Temple, Alijah, and Gabriel. They, like those before us, have been charged with securing the promise of prosperity for future generations. I hope that the following pages will be read with objectivity, and absorbed in the spirit of the original intent for which they were written as responsibility remains fundamental to uplift and *friendship is essential to the soul!*

Dr. A. Yager Wyatt   12.2014

Reader's Guide

"It's not the style that motivates me, as much as an attitude of openness that I have when I go into a project."

Herbie Hancock

Since my college days, I've done all of my studying to Jazz. I've found it to be pleasing and effective for occupying enough of my brain to maintain a level of enjoyable concentration, without drifting. So, in keeping with my tradition and for breaking the monotony of a comprehensive presentation to various readers, I have used the classifications described earlier with icons and explanations on the following pages.

"Jazz music should be inclusive. Smooth jazz to me rules out a certain kind of drama and a certain tension that I think all music needs. Especially jazz music, since improvising is one of the cornerstones of what jazz is. And when you smooth it out, you take all the drama out of it."

David Sanborn

Not Too Deep is like smooth jazz. It's just enough to be relevent to what you are doing at the time. But, it doesn't get in the way.

Readers Guide

"Knowledge is freedom and ignorance is slavery"

Miles Davis

Deep is like Miles. Regardless of the type of jazz he was exploring, he gave the audience enough of it through his presentation to be able to identify.

"There is never any end... There are always new sounds to imagine; new feelings to get at. And always, there is the need to keep purifying these feelings and sounds so that we can really see what we've discovered in its pure state."

John Coltrane

Real Deep is like 'Trane. If you paid attention, he would take you all the way through a composition, and in every direction. As fulfilling as it may have been, you would also probably have been tired.

Introduction

The direction of policy makers for resolving the United States' (US) health care crisis, including disparity reduction (Barton, 2010), has remained prominent within government backed proposals (Bloomrosen & Detmer, 2010). Further, it has been projected that by 2050, the ethnic populations of the US will double to approximately 40% of the overall population. This is to include African Americans who currently make up roughly 13% (Montague & Perchonok, 2007; US Census Bureau, 2014).

Following initiatives that were implemented during the African American Civil Rights Movement (US Department of Health and Human Services [HHS], 2014), an attention to African American disparities was brought forth in a HHS report entitled "Health, United States, 1983." That report acknowledged the gap between our community population versus others for death and illness. In support, The Task Force on Black Minority Health subsequently followed with a 1985 analytical report (National Center for Health Statistics, 2009). Given the current national cultures respecting academics, research, and applied health, these objectives have defined key factors for establishing vested provider-community partnerships with meaningful use through evidence-based medicine, or EBM (Cliff, 2012). This was based on evidence that demonstrated the expected benefits to be gained from the adoption of health information technology (HIT) by providers and consumers would remain proportional to their financial, ethical, and moral investments (McClellan, Casalino, Shortell, & Rittenhouse, 2013).

Respecting African Americans, the resource pool of health providers made available for disparity-reduction has remained limited (Kreuter et al., 2011). It has been concluded that comprehensive solutions for improvements must include initiatives targeted at their underserved communities, and responsibly aimed at meeting their needs through the workforce development goals embedded within the Health Information Technology for Economic and Clinical Health ACT, or HITECH (HHS, 2009; Kreuter et al., 2011). These factors have remained vital to strategic plans, and have allowed organizational leaders to mitigate market forces while attempting to achieve goals (Buchbinder & Shanks, 2012).

But, solutions to this dynamic have been compounded by insufficient or non-inclusive African-American buy-ins to science and health technology (Hernandez et al., 2012; Valla & Williams, 2012). Studies have determined that future educational and career models for all pre and post-graduates must reflect the needs specific to defined workforce roles of aspiration (Buchbinder & Shanks, 2012; Hersh, 2010). There has remained a need to modify the exposure, recruitment, and attrition schemes throughout the entire educational spectrum related to desired pre-requisites for wide-spread HIT adoption

(Hurd et al., 2013; James et al., 2012; Kreuter et al., 2011; McClellan et al., Muller et al., 2010).

Supported by HITECH, the federal government has backed its initiatives for better outcomes and disparity reduction with adoption incentives (Bloomrosen & Detmer, 2010; Hersh, 2010). Most of us in the health system are aware that over 19 billion dollars of incentives aimed at HIT implementations have been provided. Inherent to these approaches has been the practice of patient-first treatment for improved trust, acceptance, and compliance. However, it has been shown that goals will not be realized without the development of vested providers as adoptive leaders for internal and external change (National Center for Healthcare Leadership, Institute for Diversity in Health Management, American Hospital Association, & American College of Healthcare Executives, 2004).

Comprehensive strategies for building providers as vested community stakeholders has remained to be developed at grass-roots levels, i.e. educational, research, and post-graduate (Hersh & Wright, 2010). And though leadership qualities have often proven to be intrinsic (Borkowsi, 2009), it has been shown that they can be learned through adequate cultural exposure and re-enforcement (Cummings et al., 2013; Hernandez et al., 2012; Hurd et al, 2012). As a result, a conclusive need for realistic strategies towards work-force development for projected HIT usages has remained (Hersh &

Wright, 2008). For African American communities, cultural patterns coupled with methods for educational and career development have needed to be modified through students, educators, and mentors (Hurd, Sánchez, Zimmerman, & Caldwell, 2013). Similar initiatives for embedded career aspirations have proven the potential yield of stakeholders vested in these objectives and targeted towards reducing the disparities common to *their* ethnic communities (James, Starks, Segrest, & Burke, 2012; Ofili et al., 2014).

To exemplify, my parents lived in the southeast section of Washington, DC during my birth. At the age of 3, our family moved from there to Glenarden, MD. I was raised in that community during my formative years, until I left at the age of 18 to pursue my undergraduate studies at Hampton Institute, now University. The majority of my closest in age cousins remained in the district and our visiting exchanges were weekly, if not daily, at various times. My community, as I remember it, was over 95% African American. This included our mayor, professionals, adopted neighborhood parents, spiritual, educational, youth activity leadership and mentors. Many of them were one-in-the-same. That was how it stayed until my first real exposures to cultural diversity occurred at our neighborhood elementary school, when mostly white kids were bused in for integration.

For us collectively, our culture of capability through our pre-existing resources had already been instilled in us through living proof. True, we may have been ignorant to the equitable distribution of physical resources that were necessary and thankfully afforded through integration. But, that is not the point I am trying make at this time. We had a network of community re-enforcement and confidence that was instilled in us from our early beginnings and that we've continued to carry throughout life's journey. That was our *cultural system*. In addition, for us living within the Washington, DC-metropolitan area, African American leadership was not only commonplace from our young perspectives towards budding aspirations; it was the norm for achieving those goals through community support.

At that time, though our environment proved to be nurturing and appreciably middle-class by *our* standards, Prince George's County was one of the poorest in the state of Maryland. Out of that setting for my Hood fraternity of brothers, i.e. over 45 years of friendship since pre-school, came a NASA engineer; 2 professional counselors of education and public health; a circuit court judge; an information technology (IT) professional; a law enforcement officer; and me. Further, more recent history has recorded Prince George's County as being the most affluent county in the nation to hold an African-American majority population (*Chappell, 2006;* Howell, 2006). As husbands, fathers, and homemakers, we've all left *our* neighbor-*hood*. But we all come back, physically, spiritually, and emotionally through an engrained sense of belonging. I have remained proud to be a part of them and our culture. I like go-go, Dougie Fresh quarterback jerseys, hoodies, hoop, and Jazz. I like Hains Point, Sandy Point, half-smokes, and doin' it at the park. Oh yeah, all of it. And, that aspect should serve to exemplify the necessity for *centrality* and *identification* that has been expressed in this book's latter passages (Sellers, Shelton, Rowley, and Chavous, 1998).

Collectively, our lives have suffered all of the common hurdles, i.e. highest-highs and lowest-lows, of our generational peers. However, considering current national trends, I think we can consider ourselves to have obtained appreciable levels of success towards remaining productive family, community, and social assets. In the broader sense, we have remained vested stakeholders. We are but some of many with similar stories produced from traditional African American communities to be exemplified nationwide. But, just as it has been so for our nation's health care system, our African American community system for vested-social development, growth, and sustained prosperity has remained fragmented in thought, ambition, and resource availability to a critical level of inefficiency.

With due respect given to the monumental achievements recorded within *Brown vs. Board of Education* of 1954 (US Courts, 2014); being born in 1964, I have often bench-marked the latter era as ours being the first generation of African Americans to have been provided *comprehensive* government-backed legislation for securing educational, health, and economic resources. The Civil Rights Act afforded us tools that we could attempt to use advantageously, regardless of the remaining racial barriers yet to be addressed. From that, a personal responsibility to make good on the sacrifices of others who suffered for those gains has held. Additionally, my relationships with African American colleagues throughout my career have again proven that I am only one of many of us from all professions that have shared this self-imposed responsibility. As a whole, they have and continue to represent well as professional foot-soldiers of responsibility for the betterment of our communities.

However, it was reported in a NY Times article that as of 2013, approximately 5% of the nation's physicians and dentists were black (Schwartz & Cooper, 2013). Further, only 3.9% of lawyers, 3% of architects, and 1% were chief executives of US Fortune 500 companies were black, although estimated accounts for African Americans of the working-age population was 12%. As those are but a few examples respecting the totality of professional career alternatives, these figures have yet to improve for over 20 years (Holmes, 2005; Schwartz & Cooper, 2013). As a community-vested African American health care professional, my socially instilled belief that *achievement is fundamental to responsible outreach* (AFRO) has remained.

Respecting that, this book was drafted in supportive argument for more solutions aimed at the early incorporation of informatics within entire community spectrums for the development of required pre-requisites, coupled with proven cultural patterns needed for success (Kotter, 2007; Hersh & Wright, 2010). In doing so, it was my wish for this book to serve as a general reference for grounding the initial exposure of readers to the fields of informatics, their potentials as pathways for personal or professional development, and HIT supported economic growth. This reference has included:

▲ Descriptions for key legal, regulatory, and ethical issues impacted by information technology.
▲ Explanations, language definitions, terminology, ontology, and acronyms related to informatics supported disparity reduction.
▲ The identification of proven personal, community, organizational needs and readiness methods towards HIT adoption.
▲ The identification of alternative career paths inherent to needs associated with informatics for the ongoing support of disparity reduction in the nation's African American population.

Evidence has suggested that national initiatives need to be developed collaboratively through solutions of diversity (Hersh & Wright, 2010; Kreuter et al., 2011). In support, I have used literature review methods to identify studies that showed more research was warranted for developing effective educational infrastructures for informatics within our communities (Hersh & Wright, 2010; Joshi, Puricelli Perin, 2012, Kampov-Polevoi, & Hemminger, 2011).

Table of Contents

Fragmentation: Our Health System 1

Health Status: US versus Global 7

Informatics: Importance..................................19

Informatics: Nutz & Boltz........................29

Treatment Uses.....................................51

Funding Better Medicine 59

Informatics Systems Management...........................71

IS Finance, Implementation & Maintenance......79

Architecture & Infrastructure..............................95

Organizational Needs..................................109

Cultures of Inclusion..................................123

AFRO Education 135

AFRO Self..143

AFRO Change...151

AFRO Plan...165

AFRO Action 175

Postface 181

End Notes...183

Index..269

Chapter One ▲
Fragmentation: Our Health System

"History will tell the tale.
There's a movement about us—some young
guys, that's kinda like the quietest revolution
in jazz that I've ever heard of in my life.
And, it's amazing because
there are a group of young musicians
who definitely have vision."

● Terrance Blanchard

Nature

As emphasized by the Committee on the Quality of Health Care in America (2001), the general US health care method has been a collection of fragmented parts attempting to function, or coexist. This fragmentation, compounded by the current debates between socialism and free market values, has resulted in the escalation of health care cost, diminished quality of care, and large disparities of delivery systems between the disenfranchised and more empowered populations (Barton, 2010; Moskowitz, Guthrie, & Bindman, 2012). In order to raise quality of care levels with reduced dysfunction for financial stability, effective health care reform of the US delivery system has been called for (Committee on Quality of Health Care in America, 2001).

Philosophy

A major hurdle in the nation's reform of health care has been rooted in society's ongoing debate of care responsibility (Figure 1.1). Self-interest or past vested groups have favored competitive free market practices (Leatherman et al., 2003). Traditionally, and in contrast to other nations, our society has opted to allow the responsibility of health care needs to rest solely on the individual (Barton, 2010).

Figure 1.1

Free-market vs. Universal Coverage

As health care costs have continued to escalate and population cultures have trended towards preventive care, a demand for the research and development of socially responsible universal strategies has risen (Subramania et al., 2012). Regardless of the moralistic stance taken respecting free- market interests versus socialism, the need for reform to stabilize the escalating cost and financial burden as a nation has been driven by the data (Committee on Quality of Health Care in America, 2001). The acknowledgement that perceived poorer health statuses have significantly increased the cost and utilization of health services coupled with inefficiencies associated with reactionary disease or illness treatment, has made the need for shared responsibility evident.

Evidence-based Managed Care and Regulation

The acceptance of evidence-based managed care policies would go far in reducing the cost associated with the excessive utilization or duplication of expensive technology trends. As summarized by Barton (2010), these initiatives could reduce cost levels associated with delivery methods that have been subjected to free market practices at the expense of health care need and system efficiency. However, data lending evidence has proven only as effective as the policy, legislation, and stakeholders supporting it (Moskowitz et al., 2012). Further, initiatives could also improve the quality of care delivered by solo practitioners or lower income populations. This could be achieved by expanding the resources or expenses related to tech-driven remote medicine (Hebda & Czar, 2013), with policy driven regional-shared-usage and cost strategies.

Structure

The delivery of health care within the US has been controlled, in large part, by the government serving as the major payer (Barton, 2010; Leatherman et al., 2003). By funding or paying for approximately 50% of the nation's health care cost, the government has been targeted as the principal policy maker while shouldering the majority of blame and frustration held by those of us who've remained disgruntled with the system's make-up. For obvious reasons, this cannot continue. What began historically as post-war initiatives formed to address the health care shortages of the mid to late 1940's industrial rebuilding (Barton, 2010), has transformed into modern day dysfunction of many of those funding programs (DeLia, Hoover & Cantor, 2012). This, along with the large disparities of health care between various populations (Moskowitz, Guthrie, & Bindman, 2012), has forced the need for all constituencies of the US health delivery system to re-examine their respective focuses, while working together to development meaningful strategies of reform (Committee on Quality of Health Care in America, 2001).

Governance

The Hill Burton Act of 1946, Medicare and Medicaid were borne out of the government's self imposed social responsibility for broadening access-to-care while serving free-market and moralistically interests respectively (Barton, 2010). The nation's current health care dilemma has again required its focus in developing all-inclusive solutions of legislative policy (Goodwin & Anderson, 2012; HHS, 2009). The interests of all parties need to be represented, respected, and reflected accordingly within policy-driven legislation and stakeholder support (Figure 1.2).

Figure 1.2

Chapter Two ▲▼▲
Health Status: US versus Global

"Artistic achievements speak across epochs to people of what has been attained. It's like collective wisdom. And, it survives whatever a, a contemporary perspective or whatever it is, whatever adjustments you have to make to include yourself. It survives that. And Jazz will, will survive that also."

● Wynton Marsalis

Overview

Much of the media's focus within the nation related to research, treatment and preventive health practices has been dedicated to the emergence of infectious diseases. However, heart disease and cancer have remained the primary causes of death in the US (Centers for Disease Control [CDC], 2014a). In addition to implementing strategies that focus on promoting healthier life-style practices and community development, health care administrators have held a continued focus on those causes. Serious consideration should continue to be given to the fact that the US trails other countries respecting health status levels and treatment outcomes, despite having outspent some by twice as much. The allocation of financial resources remains to be administered with the responsibility of reflecting sound practices (Goodwin & Anderson, 2012).

But, as has been demonstrated successfully by other countries, the need for efficient and cyclic reform is as plain as it is conceivable (Barton, 2010; Institute of Medicine [IOM], 2001). To serve as examples respecting disparity reduction trends, comparisons have been drawn between the US, Canada, and the United Kingdom due to the latter two's ability to demonstrate more favorable health status reports while sacrificing less financially (World Health Organization [WHO], n.d.).

Health Indicators

Though the chances of the US mimicking Canada's single-payer system have been reduced, a comparison of two common health indicators will be demonstrated. Data trends from both examples have served to contrast the effectiveness of a free-market dominated system versus one of managed care (CDC, 2014; WHO, n.d.).

Infant Mortality

As a health status indicator, a country's infant death rate has been traditionally calculated. This aspect respecting the overall health status of populations has proven tied to the technological advancements in the care of newborns, improved environments, and living conditions (Barton, 2010; CDC, 2010). According to the World Health Organization (WHO), data has shown an infant mortality rate in Canada and the United Kingdom of 5 per 1,000 live births for both sexes, as compared to 7 per 1,000 in the US (WHO, n.d.). For African Americans in the US, infant mortalities were reported to be twice the rate of those for other groups as recent as 2006 (CDC, 2010).

Life Expectancy

Although the US life expectancy has increased over the last century, it still remains lower than many other countries that offer universal coverage while contributing significantly less of their gross domestic product (GDP) towards systemic health care (Barton, 2010; CDC, 2013). According to the WHO, the average life expectancy of 78 years within the US has remained lower than the average of 79 years in the United Kingdom, and 81 years in Canada (WHO, n.d.). For African Americans in the US, the average life expectancy has been reported to be just 75 years, or equivalent to the rate for White Americans 30 years ago (CDC, 2014a; CDC, 2014b; Friedman, 2014). Heart, cancer, stroke, and diabetic diseases have remained the primary culprits within our communities (CDC, 2014b).

As previously explained, the percentage of African American professionals from which to draw has remained small. This means that from those available, we have remained dependent upon a fraction of practicing professionals to service the needs of our collective communities with a vested interest. Further, that doesn't include the supporting professional workforce from which they are to draw. The total US African American population has been estimated to be approximately 45 million (US Census Bureau, 2012; CDC, 2012). Regardless of the cause, the inherent community development failures that have contributed to our disparities have remained of paramount concern.

Initiatives

Modern day history has seen a fragmented power struggle develop within health care and its governmental representatives. This has resulted in the realization that the amount of care demanded to sustain the health status of the nation has exhausted our resources. A respectable level of common ground needs to be reached in support of evidence-based managed care policies. New legislation, influenced predominantly by the Affordable Care Act, or ACA (Goodwin, 2012), was initiated on the principles of addressing the shortages in delivery schemes, while being conscious of financial concerns. These have included waste or mismanagement, and been supported by analytical data (Bernard et al. 2012). However, in the interest of financial health or sustainability for tax-paying customers and their actual (hands on) health care providers, a national focus should remain on building upon those achievements, i.e. the securing of expanded coverage, while aggressively aiming future modifications at supplier regulations for cost-containment.

Hospitals, Clinics and Providers

A re-evaluation of practice purpose coupled with a philosophical shift back towards the roots of delivery and hospital development may be beneficial in raising health status levels. Medical organizations within the US and abroad have proven valuable for increasing the level of doctor-patient communication (Handfield-Jones, & Kocha, 1999). They've also been effective in partnering with other organizations to address disparities within, and outside of, the profession (American Medical Association [AMA], 2008).

This has been demonstrated by community organizations with respect to the global confrontation of other epidemics (Schaetti et al., 2012; WHO, n.d.) They've proven this by refocusing some of the agenda away from free-market competitive strategies towards cost-sharing strategies with increased treatment deliveries. Therefore, the potential impact on the nation's epidemic of health care dysfunction by local chapters at US community levels of the system is strong.

Safety and Quality Assurance

Quality has been defined as the right care, at the right time with the most effective outcomes (Clancy, 2009; IOM, 2014). It and safety are essential ingredients to systemic strategies for increasing health status levels within the US, while reducing cost (IOM, 2001; Barton, 2010). Equally important are the disparities suffered by the over 5 million, mostly minority, residents of the US territories that have not been well represented in national reports on health care equity and quality (Nunez-Smith et al., 2011). In response to studies that showed an average death rate, due mostly to systemic flaws, of 98 thousand patients per year (IOM, 1999), hospitals have recently focused on safety and quality assurance in their efforts to promote patient-first delivery systems, improved treatment outcomes, and decreased expenditures (Barton, 2010). Following, attention has been drawn to strategic examples, challenges, and common barriers to implementation.

Challenges

A 2002 study identifying medical-error reporting factors which were applied to a Factor Relevance Matrix, and readily adaptable to any health setting, revealed that lack of data respecting error occurrences to be the primary impediment (Uribe, Schweikhart, Pathak, Dow, & Marsh, 2002). In 2006, survey methodology of health care respondents was used to identify the lack of systemic managerial support and resources for implementation as significant challenges (McFadden, Stock, & Gowen, 2011). Both studies identified the culturally-based impediments of litigation fear and blame towards providers, as systemic perceptive-barriers which have been proved harder to reduce without cultural shifts.

Licensure Boards

Respecting health care, the individual practices of providers are governed by state and national oversight. Requirements are monitored through their respective professional agencies and licensure boards, regardless of whether they are part of larger organizations. Professional standard-of-care practices are expected (Barton, 2010; Virginia Department of Health Professions [VDHP], 2013), and guided yearly by benchmarks for continuing education.

These initiatives are designed to keep providers in good standing with respect to those organizations.

The Joint Commission

Until recently, health organizations had no data to evaluate safety and treatment outcomes. To address this need, the Joint Commission (JC) was established in 2007 to standardize safety and quality assurance practices for its participants (Barton, 2010; Longo, Hewitt, Ge, & Schubert, 2007). JC aims for improvement and care expectancies by establishing universal standards of acceptance for its accredited participants. Accreditation has remained voluntary and their surveys have incorporated un-announced on-site facility visits. Approximately 82% of the hospitals within the United States are now JC accredited participants (Joint Commission [JC], 2013; Schmaltz, Williams, Chassin, Loeb, & Wachter, 2011).

Its general purpose has been to note areas of effectiveness and for possible improvements in the spirit of continuous quality improvement, or CQI (JC, 2013). Grown from IOM strategies for transparent patient-first deliveries, JC results are rooted in evidence-based strategies, often through supplemental publications (IOM, 2001; JC, 2013). Data has identified schemes for prioritizing and barriers (McFadden, Stock, & Gowen, 2011). They have delivered high performance trends, and research has shown the effectiveness of JC accreditation on various health care facilities (Longo, Hewitt, Ge, & Schubert, 2007; Schmaltz et al., 2011).

Successful improvements have been proven through cultural-shifts and in partnership with care-seekers' trust.

Patient Safety Indicators

Informatics tied to Patient Safety Indicators (PSI) has been defined. These initiatives have been expressed through the Agency of Healthcare Research and Quality (AHRQ). PSI implementations have significantly better reports of safety and quality assurance than those without (Menachemi, Saunders, Chukmaitov, Matthews, & Brooks, 2007).

US Territories

The Centers for Medicare & Medicaid Services (CMS) developed initiatives to measure the hospital outcomes of US territories (Centers for Medicare & Medicaid Services [CMS], n.d.; Nunez-Smith et al., 2011). Results of these initiatives have proven the need for inclusion of these territories in strategic US safety and quality assurance assessments (Nunez-Smith et al., 2011).

Continuum of Care

The health continuum of care within the US includes: promotion and prevention; primary; specialty; out-patient and acute hospital; tertiary; intensive physical rehabilitation; long-term; palliative care and hospice (IOM, 1999; IOM 2001). These have shown to be influenced by geography, health status of those populations, provider availability, and access. A need for delivery strategies that reflect the true needs of specific groups and targeted underserved populations has remained. The potential value for reducing the dysfunction displayed by rural, isolated, or disenfranchised care continuums has been accepted. All represent boxed populations of collective fragmentation. Variations of the continuum will be displayed by comparisons between rural or remote areas versus metropolitan and urban settings, to show how strategies must be adapted.

Continuum Variations

Primary care physicians, physician's aides and nurses have remained at the core of health care delivery, especially within rural settings. However, the ability for administrators to develop strategies for sufficient provider and specialty support is heavily influenced by geographic location, facility funding and population income levels. In general, the trend of recent medical graduates towards specialty care, the associated fee or salary scales, and their impact on projected career paths for those professionals have reduced the resource availability of providers respecting rural or remote areas (Barton, 2010; Hersh & Wright, 2010).

Strategies which use national prevalence and trends data to identify local risk factors (CDC, 2010) need to be coupled with the appropriate use of community, private resources, and governmental incentives that directly impact the population's health status (Trust for America's Health, 2012). This has been demonstrated by community hospitals that have established a focus on ambulatory care while taking on the expanded role of serving as an on-site resource for wellness programs, preventive education and physical rehabilitation (Johnson, Murphy, McNeese, Reddy, & Purao, 2013). These organizations have relied on tech-supported remote deliveries and tertiary, or educational hospitals, to fulfill specialty needs that may be otherwise unaffordable (Tan, 2008; Hebda & Czar, 2013). Coupled with community partnerships and government programs for preventive education, risk-factor reduction, and palliative care; these models should be noted in the strategic development of others for the analysis of a population's health status trends, and responding with efficient on-site and remote care (Nee et al., 2008).

Potential Career Alternatives:

Global Health
Informatics

Epidemiology
Informaticist

Public Health
Informatics

Public Health
Informatician

Chapter Three ▲▼▲

Informatics: Importance

"A lot of people ask me where music is going today. I think it's going in short phrases. If you listen, anybody with an ear can hear that. Music is always changing. It changes because of the times and the technology that's available, the material that things are made of, like plastic cars instead of steel. So when you hear an accident today it sounds different, not all the metal colliding like it was in the forties and fifties. Musicians pick up sounds and incorporate that into their playing, so the music that they make will be different."

● Miles Davis

Overview

To be demonstrated in latter pages, Informatics has proven its worth as a sub-discipline to various fields through the immediacy of shared knowledge it affords. Respecting health, the value of informatics lay within the creative, dynamic, and ever-expanding possibilities of merging, or replacing, traditional means of treatment delivery, documentation, and communication with technology. The objective has been to afford unparallel patient safety, compliance, and health provider efficiency while reducing misdiagnosis, treatment, and organizational errors in a general scope (IOM, 2001; HHS, 2014b).

Patient and provider benefits have included the reduction of radiographic exposure suffered. This has been achieved through the utilization of digital imaging (Patel, 2010). This technology has allowed for multiple images to be produced immediately, thereby increasing the number of visual diagnostic aids available to the practitioner at a fraction of the traditional exposure rate of film (Gackowski et al., 2011; Patel, 2010). Another has been the increased availability, accuracy, and speed-of-delivery of documented information made available electronically between multiple providers, consultants, researchers, and specialists for increased communication and support (Kawamoto, Lobach, Willard, & Ginsburg, 2009; Pevnick et al., 2012).

Social Impact

"Culturally we are abloom in a new field, but it is yet decidedly a question as to what we shall reap—a few flowers or a harvest. That depends upon how we cultivate this art of the drama in the next few years."

— Alain Locke

Professor Locke was referring to the progression of African-American theatre during his era (Molesworth, 2012). Similarly, implications from current and future informatics integrations have yet to be defined. Strategic expansions into informatics have supported the cultural shift within health, academic, and social systems towards personal, community, and organization responsibility. History has shown us that despite the hiccups inherent to the initial exploration into usages of scientific, medical, and technological advances, society has traditionally benefited from the learned experiences gained from the initial good intent of those applications. Medical implants, i.e. prosthetic and dental, have served as prime examples (Patel, 2010).

As tablets, smart-phones, and free video conferencing have become social norms, the possibility for the "standard-of-care" to include the dedication of secure HIT supported public networks for optimizing access to care and useful information is realistic (Englebardt & Nelson, 2002; Montague & Perchonok, 2012). Reducing the associated community, organizational, and social roadblocks of cost and delivery has proven achievable at various levels (Montague & Perchonok, 2012). The implications for expanding upon those dynamics have remained far reaching and invaluable to those of the underserved populations (McNeill, Puleo, Bennett, & Emmons, 2007; Montague & Perchonok, 2012). HIT approaches have been designated as the tool of choice for our communities to combat exceedingly high rates of cardiovascular diseases, diabetes, asthma, and cancer (Montague & Perchonok, 2012).

IOM Recommendations

The national focus was drawn to improving the quality and safety of US health care deliveries as a result of two monumental reports and recommendations, offered through the Institute of Medicine (IOM) between 1999 and 2001. Those reports identified medical error as a significant causative agent for health care related deaths at a high rate (IOM, 1999), and initiated several changes to health care systems in an attempt to avoid such occurrences in the future (IOM, 2001). Following is a description of the benefits and challenges for reporting medical errors and HIT integration, based upon IOM recommendations (IOM, 1999; Wachter, 2010).

The IOM identified the safe, effective, timely and equitable distribution of patient-first treatment deliveries as fundamental objectives for health care providers (IOM, 2001). Strategies to improve medical error reporting supported the past theories of total quality management (TQM) and continuous improvement (CQI) while attempting to utilize more efficient means for identifying and correcting medical mistakes, i.e. avoidable, preventive, and post-operatively (Varkey, 2010). To meet the IOM's call for the development of a health care infrastructure based on evidence-based practice, or EBP (IOM, 1999), transparency through sound open-disclosure report strategies has remained vital to its success (Wachter, 2004).

Through its recommendations, the IOM has supported the theory that automated clinical information and feedback should deliver the promise of improved outcomes (IOM, 2001). Improvements to quality measurements and adverse events for evaluation have proved challenging, as administrators have been tasked with implementing new safety protocols while attempting to raise the required competency levels of the workforce to be charged with making proper assessments (Varkey, 2010). Health care system administrators and developers have needed to remain focused on maximizing the correct utilization of the input related to IOM indentified priority conditions (IOM, 2001), for the staged-building of reliable infrastructures upon which future expansion may occur with confidence. With the underlying purpose being to identify deficiencies for quality and safety improvements (IOM, 2001), the challenge remains in the ability for health care systems to strike a careful balance between effective systems of reporting and accountability without excessive admonishment (Galt &Paschal, 2011).

Informatics: Importance

Overview of Informatics

The institutional impacts for generating stakeholders respecting technology and sciences have remained dispersed throughout entire spectrum of education, research, and health related fields (National Academy of Engineering, 2014). The early exposure would provide a vehicle for alternative career paths towards the overall goal of disparity reduction regardless of which informatics field is chosen, because the fundamental pre-requisites for those careers would also have been established.

Fields

Discipline options for informatics entry are wide-spread and globally reaching. As explained through the Journal of Education, Informatics, and Cybernetics (2014), academic leadership goals have included the bi-directional exchange of original research, reflections, and educational reviews. Marine biologists have called for the strategic integration of databases for sharing information between oceanographers (Vanden Berghe, Appeltans, Costello, & Pissierssens, 2004). Ecologists have targeted collaborative solutions towards environmental sustainability through informatics (International Conference on Ecological Informatics, 2014). The National Aeronautics and Space Administration (NASA) has called for the open and collaborative innovation of informatics applications for their professional use, as well as for school children, teachers, parents, and the general public (NASA, 2013; Top Coder, 2012). Further, the field of sports informatics (SI) has become embedded within athletic organizations (Institute of Training Science and Sport Informatics, 2006; Zhang & Su Liu, 2004). And, medical forensics and criminologists have been relying on its potential to hurdle challenges inherent to DNA matching or case solving (Center for Advanced Forensics, 2014; Morancea & Costin, 2008). These are but a few examples. However, the remainder of this text will draw focus to the potentials for integrating educational, health professional, and medical informatics applications towards disparity reductions, and respecting those areas of concern towards economic stability and sustained prosperity.

Patient-Centered Care

Adam's ARTHouse©

"I hate straight singing. I have to change a tune to my own way of doing it. That's all I know."
— Billie Holiday

Evidence has proven that health care delivery systems have traditionally fallen short of patient expectations, i.e. lack of information, communication, and attentiveness to comfort (Varkey, 2010; HHS, 2013). Referred to throughout health organizations as patient-centered care, health organizations have responded by attempting to build patient-first strategies towards addressing these concerns. These have been represented through survey initiatives known as the Hospital Consumer Assessment of Healthcare Providers and Systems, and the Consumer Assessment of Healthcare Providers and Systems, or HCAHPS and CAHPS (Varkey, 2010). Despite this focus, analysis of measures reported for many hospitals coupled with national averages have fallen short of our health care's desired systemic goals (HHS, 2013). Provider responsiveness has proven proportional to patient trust in provider-patient relationships. To have this reflected in patient feedback by higher percentage rates of satisfaction has been a common goal, i.e. internally among facilities and nationally (Aragon, Richardson, Lawrence, & Gesell, 2013; HHS, 2013). As expressed earlier respecting continuum improvements (IOM, 2001), the lack of information and continuity of care has often proven a barrier to a patient's *sense* of security (Varkey, 2010).

Potential Career Alternatives:

Eco-informaticist

Environmental
Informatics

Environmental
Data Scientist

NASA
Climate
Informaticist

NASA
Cloud Strategist

NASA
Bio-Informatics

Medical Forensic
Informatics

Sports Informatics

Ocean Biodiversity
Informatics

Chapter Four ▲▼▲
Informatics: Nutz & Boltz

Overview

The branches stemming from health and medical informatics applications aimed at better treatment methods have extended throughout organizations of academic, research, and care delivery. The following pages provide fundamental definitions and explain associated applications. Focus has also been drawn to direct relationships between those uses and common areas of concern respecting diseases that have remained inherent to the African American populations.

Measurements

Health care measurements provide data to be evaluated for increased quality and safety (HHS, 2013). Over the past several years, there has been a national and international increase of interest towards developing successful strategies for measuring related outcomes (Varkey, 2010). In response, patient reported outcome (PRO) measures, i.e. status assessments, symptoms, patient care satisfaction, and etc., have been employed through various survey tools to collect data and information that has accurately reflected these outcomes for comparisons and improvements (Chen, Ou, & Hollis, 2013). Proven measures must be reliable, relevant, feasible, and applicable to improvement strategies.

Cancer

"I want to be able to help other people do this. I want to give them the chance. Because, if I hadn't been blessed to the point I've been blessed, then I couldn't do this. You know what's disheartening? So many people, even in Oklahoma, leave it on and die. A lot of people don't have the insurance I had. A lot of people don't have the money to go through that."
— Wayman Tisdale.

Former NBA player and renowned smooth jazz bassist Wayman Tisdale said those words in an interview shortly before his death from cancer, as he sat in a chair without his prosthetic right leg. The 44-year old cancer victim established a vehicle for hope through his foundation that was begun in the mist of his battle with the disease (Carlson, 2009). Like many other African Americans, cancer impacts to me and my loved ones have remained too common a family occurrence. Improvements to cancer treatment deliveries through measured feedback have been documented.

One study specifically rated the usefulness, effectiveness and impact of traditionally used PROs in cancer patients within an oncology setting (Chen, Ou, & Hollis, 2013). The management of bench-marked outcomes has proven to be best performed closest to the care itself, i.e. problem and departmentally focused (HHS, 2013). The unique treatment dynamics, to include adverse effects or disease progression, makes the evaluation of traditional PRO measurement practices towards cancer patient management an identifiable need (Chen, Ou, & Hollis, 2013). In addition, a common barrier to data usefulness has been the misuse of quality measures towards varied applications or to reflect misleading outcomes, i.e. statistics (Hawkes & Marsh, 2004).

To evaluate the effectiveness of past PRO measurements, a mixed methodology search was performed to identify 27 relevant studies over an 11 year period. The study revealed that though there appeared to be many PRO measurement strategies applied during this time-frame, their effectiveness specific to cancer outcomes remained unclear due to the lack of applications applied in actual oncology settings. Results supported the widely adopted conclusion in health care that PROs improved generalized patient-centered care. However, for accurate bench-mark assessments of patient-centered outcomes, more focused measures of specified cancer treatment characteristics within oncology settings are needed for proper outcome evaluation (Chen, Ou, & Hollis, 2013). Findings of this type have continued to highlight the ongoing importance for like-studies respecting cancer research and treatments within African American communities.

Genetic Variants

"In practice it is possible to determine directly the skin colour and hence the ethnic affiliations of the ancient Egyptians by microscopic analysis in the laboratory; I doubt if the sagacity of the researchers who have studied the question has overlooked the possibility."
— Cheikh Anta Diop

As a scientist, anthropologist, and physicist, Dr. Diop championed African identity in the historical context of human origination through an evidence-based research of phenotypic expression. Much of his work was later confirmed in broader theoretical contexts through DNA studies, as he had laid the groundwork for such evidentiary approaches, i.e. melanin content and radiocarbon ratios to support cultural, philosophical and evolutionary trait theories based on empirical data. His processes were later applied to medical forensics to methodically identify the racial make-up of burn victims. Dr. Diop's work generated needed dialogue, i.e. confirmations and critics, while contributing heavily to defining patterns of significance for African origins respecting human development and causative agents (Diop, 1974; Mokhatar, 1981).

Genetic variants have proven impactful to the medical effectiveness of treating common diseases ranging from acquired immune deficiency syndrome (AIDS) to Alzheimer's (Cruchaga et al., 2013). By identifying unique genetic characteristics of predisposition to diseases, drug reactions, and affects, genomic data will have a significant impact on personalized medicine. Health care's future empowerment of *activated* patients and shared responsibility requires system governance to insure that implementations are beneficial to health outcomes (Özdemir et al., 2013).

Various drug hypersensitivities, i.e. abacavir in HIV patients, Stevens-Johnson syndrome, and aspirin, have been associated to human leukocyte antigen (HLA) gene variants (Guéant, et al., 2008). The integration of identifiable predicators linked to HLA variants into information systems would serve well to safeguard against damaging outcomes during E-prescribing (Ronaldson & McNeil, 2009). Its inclusion should reduce the number of accidental hypersensitivity occurrences, while enhancing processes of data mining and identifiable patterns towards treatment and prevention due to the wide range of HLA variant responses linked to disease specificity and patient ethnicity (Özdemir et al., 2013). This would contribute to regional health organizational movements as well as benefit the globalization of health exchanges between various populations (Dandara et al., 2012).

Much of the provider reluctance towards personalized medicine has been attributable to education, as genomics was either a non-discipline or a new concept during their professional education (Aspinall, & Hamermesh, 2007). Complicating matters further are pharmaceutical companies that have marketed to broad-based practices of profitability over specified treatment effects coupled with provider re-imbursements that have lacked adequate financial incentives for diagnostic testing (Kawamoto, Lobach, Willard, & Ginsburg, 2009).

The dynamics of updating or obtaining current procedural terminology (CPT) coding to correspond to advancements in personalized medicine, i.e. diagnostic test, has remained a barrier (Aspinall & Hamermesh, 2007). Another has been the amount and complexity of clinical decision support, i.e. standardization and governance, required to be developed in support of successful personalized medicine implementations (Kawamoto et al., 2009).

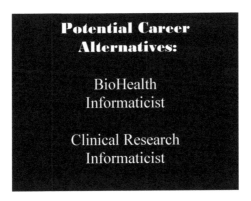

Potential Career Alternatives:

BioHealth Informaticist

Clinical Research Informaticist

Public Health

Public Health Informatics (PHI) has served to utilize computer science and technology to educate, enhance, and promote the prevention and treatment of population groups as opposed to addressing specific individualized patient needs. This has been achieved by utilizing the data afforded through informatics to respond proactively and or reactively, with knowledge gained, to disease trends and tendencies (Yasnoff, O'Carroll, Linkins & Kilbourne, 2000). Several examples of effective usages have included: simulation studies of sexually transmitted diseases in population groups; analyzing health information system implementations in developing countries; analyzing the potential of successful e-prescribing within the current environment of health reform; and real-time reporting of public health threats (CDC, 2014a; WHO, n.d.).

An important aspect of the informatics supporting these tasks are Community Health Status Indicators (CHSI), which have served as data resources for monitoring, analyzing, and targeting community health strategies. Through CHSI, many organizations have collaborated, including federal and private agencies, to provide data initiatives, research, and evidence-based policy development (National Information Center on Health Services Research and Health Care Technology [NICHSR], 2010). The uses have spanned various disciplines and have inherited the challenges characteristic to successful merges across diverse platforms, while reducing security and privacy issues. Therefore, the participation of public health professionals with respect to design dialogue and implementation (Mensah, 2012), coupled with the standardization of infrastructure while raising the competency level requirements of public health professionals, has remained vital (Yasnoff, et al., 2000).

Oral Health

To serve as an example, research has proven a substantial link between diseases of the oral cavity and race, ethnicity, and poverty (Mensah, 2012). This argument was supported by the Surgeon General's report, titled *Oral Health America,* which termed the oral disease of poor children, elderly and minority groups a silent epidemic. In response, PHI has been utilized to analyze data in developmental strategies targeted towards oral health intervention. One such study, *Overcoming Data Challenges Examining Oral Health Disparities in Appalachia,* was performed to geographically analyze disparities (Krause, May, & Crossman, 2012). The study resourced data provided by the Behavioral Risk Factor Surveillance System (BRFSS); a collaborative effort of CHSI between the CDC and state health departments focusing on behaviors and conditions linked to major causes of death (NICHSR, 2008). The results produced various means by which data being provided by the BRFSS can be utilized and interpreted more effectively by dental health care professionals in developing strategies of prevention and treatment delivery options (Krause, 2012).

Respecting African American oral health, Slaughter and Evans (2007) argued for an increased responsibility within our communities concerning older members. Their studies proved the potential for culturally tailored presentations through a conceptual framework called the *MAP-IT* technique. However, the oral health status levels within our communities have continued to lag appreciably (Dye, Li, & Thornton-Evans, 2012). Further, the National Institute of Dental and Craniofacial Research (NIDCR) has recognized educational disparities respecting the higher risk for oral cancer in African American men through their initiatives (NIDCR, 2014). Collectively, all serve to demonstrate the potential for informatics supported actions towards reducing these disparities.

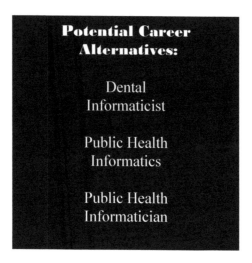

Potential Career Alternatives:

Dental Informaticist

Public Health Informatics

Public Health Informatician

Health IT Approaches

HIT offers the promise of real-time shared communication of medical information for quality assurance and patient safety (IOM, 2001). The allergy documentation, high-risk alerts, and prescription regimens offered through medical technology has supported the promise for clinical decision support levels traditionally unimaginable (Hebda & Czar, 2013). Staff reduction and re-organization; process improvement; and streamlined billing with reduced error and unpaid services have remained key objectives of national reform (Payne et al., 2013).

The legal liability and waste associated with duplicate or improper treatment have remained paramount to cost containment strategies (Arlotto, Birch, Crockett, & Irby, 2007). Remote HIT approaches have been aimed at closing the access-to-care gap while enhancing quality assurance through provider communications (Hebda & Czar, 2013). Quality assurance as proven tightly linked to standardized regulatory metrics targeted towards regulatory and financial incentives (Moskowitz, Guthrie, & Bindman, 2012). With respect to administrative error-based cost containment, the reduction of lost revenues associated with improper billing or collections have remained integral (Payne et al., 2013).

Clinical Decision Support

"It's taken me all my life to learn what not to play."
— John Birks (Dizzy) Gillespie

Clinical Decision Support (CDS) systems have served as a framework for communicating information and data to the provider with the purpose of administering better, safer and more efficient treatment to the patient. Their purpose has been to effectively merge clinical human knowledge and experience with computer technology to afford more comprehensive delivery systems (Hebda & Czar, 2013). Raising the level of application and efficiency for proven CDS systems has been shown to enhance the treatment methods and lead to more favorable outcomes throughout health care. Through the use of computer attributes such as "alerts" that may be applicable to patient allergies and medical complications, or drug interaction warnings, these systems offer an invaluable tool to be utilized by health care providers with an immediacy not afforded by traditional means of health care documentation. Other attributes include technological guidance for more accurate implementation of diagnostic and treatment tools such as radiation therapy (Abbott, 2012), and imaging (González, Carpenter, van Hemert & Wardlaw, 2010).

Successful implementation of CDS systems throughout the field of various health care organizations would reduce the number of adverse drug events and treatment errors, by severely hampering the dysfunctional methods that resulted in these events (Gurwitz, 2008). In addition to the aforementioned references made to alerts, data patterns with respect to treatment and therapeutic regimens' would be more readily identifiable as reports would become more manageable, thereby increasing user interpretation efficiency. All of these serve to aid health care providers in remaining true to treatment recommendations and guidelines by lending to more efficient time management practices (Payne, 2000).

Respecting research concerning diseases that have remained detrimental to African American communities, i.e. diabetes and heart, support for this rationale was exemplified by findings reported on behalf of the Diabetes Improvement Group-Intervention Trial (DIG-IT) which utilized a Cluster-Randomized Trial (CRT) to assist in better treatment outcomes of diabetic patients (Love et al., 2008). Further support was demonstrated and reported by the SAPHIRE hospital pilot project which focused on utilizing electronic monitoring systems in conjunction with computer technology to provide clinical decision making feedback for patients with sub-acute coronary syndromes (Nee et al., 2008). Major examples of CDS have included Computerized Physician/Provider Order Entry (CPOE), and Electronic Prescribing (E-prescribing). Both models have aided health care providers with respect to entering the orders and therapeutic instructions of health care providers into information systems of hospitals and health care organizations (Hebda & Czar, 2013).

As user and developmental infrastructure competencies have increased, effective and efficient CDS systems have started to become the norm throughout health organizations. The level of intelligence respecting provider-to-provider and provider-to-patient interactions should lend greatly to achieving better treatment outcomes.

Computerized Provider Order Entry

CPOE has come to be an indispensible tool of CDS. The ability for these systems to aid in avoiding adverse events caused by providers of cross-departmental specialties supports the IOM objectives of automated clinical data and enhanced communication (IOM, 2001). Its full implementation has been challenged by the lack of a nationally standardized continuity and alignment between systems (Hebda & Czar, 2013). The result has been adverse work-flow schemes associated with integrations of CPOE systems within some facilities (Niazkhani, Pirnejad, Berg, and Aarts, 2009).

E-prescribing

Through this electronic entry method, health care providers have communicated patient prescriptions to pharmacists and drug dispensaries. E-prescribing has served as a fundamental tool for reducing the error rates associated with pharmaceutical contraindications and provider-based drug choice inaptness (Schiff & Bates, 2000).

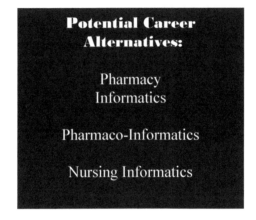

Potential Career Alternatives:

Pharmacy Informatics

Pharmaco-Informatics

Nursing Informatics

Electronic Health Records

Electronic health record (EHR) integrations have supported patient safety with legible documentation and automation (IOM, 2001). This, coupled with remote medicine, has provided access, education, and consultation for improved patient-centered treatment to and from remote locations. However, inherent to this technology is the need for securing proper strategies related to patient vulnerability, as confidential and vital information is made increasing available through web-related technology (Hebda & Czar, 2013; Wager, Lee, & Glaser, 2009).

The electronic medical record (EMR) is a digital interpretation of a medical chart or medical history from the provider's view. Providers use the EHR as a comprehensive amalgamation of the EMR and the patient health record (PHR) obtained from various sources. They have offered the ability to access and compare information that would normally be isolated or unavailable for immediate review by one or more providers through traditional means. EHRs have enhanced provider-to-provider communication during the course of coordinated treatment efforts and aided patient-to-provider communication, respecting past medical history (Finely, 2012).

Personal Health Records

PHRs and personal medical records (PMR) have progressed to include web based data portals, to include Microsoft's Health Vault. This application has allowed patients to self-manage the input and collection of data related to their medical history, as opposed to the traditional paper health history forms found within paper medical charts (Microsoft, 2014). These advancements have brought about significant social challenges respecting the logistics of implementation, security breaches, regulatory standardization, and governorship that have remained common to technological culture changes. These have remained just as relevant to African American communities (Montague & Perchonok, 2012). However, the potential benefits for advancing the overall quality of health care and accessibility have more than justified their potential worth for reducing disparities.

A focus throughout the nation's system has been the desire to collect and reference detailed amounts of health and medical histories located within networked centralized resources at private, state, and national levels. As a practicing clinician, I can attest to this goal being common to providers of all organizational aspects, to include the civilian and military sectors. These interests have served to aid in the reduction of errors resulting from the communication barriers of providers while providing a tool for increased overall efficiency respecting access, consultation, and cost (Englebardt & Nelson, 2002). This purpose has resulted in the conceptual formation and development of entities such as the Nationwide Healthcare Information Network (NwHIN) and the National Health Information Infrastructure (NHII) respectively (Marchibroda, 2004; HealtIT Dot Gov, 2014).

Benefits

The underlying objectives have been defined as the secure accessibility of desired information, in the better interest of patient treatment and research, to aid in diagnosis and disease prevention. In the broader scope, society could finally bridge the gap between access-to-care and overall prevention with meaningful and effective resources for education and treatment (Hebda & Czar, 2013; HHS, 2009).

Challenges

One concern has been in the ability to filter the information needed for the diagnosis and treatment of specific problems from the unwanted material afforded through its use (Tan & Payton, 2010). Further, initial barriers to successful implementations have included providers' reluctances towards change coupled with competency shortcomings in the clinical workplace that have resulted in workflow disruptions, end-user frustration, and lack of cohesion due to fragmentation across various facility settings (Niazkhani, Pirnejad, Berg, & Aarts, 2009).

Respecting PHRs, or PMRs, and the level of expectations for patients entering data and managing information about their past medical history, an inherent technological barrier has also remained to be addressed (Montague & Perchonok, 2012). There is a continued need for patients to become more knowledgeable about methods which may appear cumbersome to both patients and providers (Hersh & Wright, 2010; Montague & Perchonok, 2012). Collectively, the need for cultural shifts in health competency standards has remained within the realms of providers, patients, and administrative delivery systems.

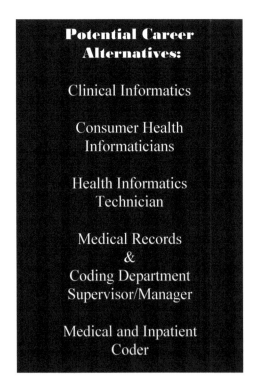

Potential Career Alternatives:

Clinical Informatics

Consumer Health Informaticians

Health Informatics Technician

Medical Records & Coding Department Supervisor/Manager

Medical and Inpatient Coder

Privacy

Perceptions associated with patient privacy have remained a concern and a barrier to cultural shifts for wide-spread consumer use. These are warranted. Due to the nature of the technology and with respect to patient vulnerability, patient-safety measures aimed at preventing the misuse of information or adverse events resulting from malfunction need to accompany integrations. Melani Cruise (personal communication, December 20, 2014), a private and organizational health care office administrator for over 20 years, and now a coding specialist for Georgetown University Hospital, concurs. Concerning needed administrative pre-requisites or competencies, throughout her career, i.e. rural and metropolitan delivery systems, she has found that the most troubling areas for future HIT implementations to be, "Maintaining the HIPAA compliance and integrity while keeping up with fast-paced technological advancement and bridging the various EMR formats to better facilitate provider communication for improved care." Respecting that, the cyclic development of strong and effective regulations and guidelines, as defined by the Health Insurance Portability and Accountability Act (HIPAA) and HITECH, for the privacy of EHRs have continued to remain necessary (McKinney, 2009; Sittig, & Singh, 2012).

HIPAA
Privacy

Established for the purpose of defining improvements to efficiency and effectiveness of heath care systems, future expansions of this act have been required to coincide with the advances inherent to the adoption of EHRs. Public awareness has been heightened through educational aids supported through informatics (HHS, 2003; HHS, 2014a). These tools should aid in lowering privacy-concern barriers to wide-spread adoption for better patient management.

HITECH
Privacy

Borne out of HIPAA's aforementioned expansion needs, this amendment has also address privacy concerns. It defined the required notification procedure for organizations respecting unsecured breaches of protected health information to the Department of Health and Human Services, i.e. within 60 days (McKinney, 2009).

NHIN and NHII

As explained earlier, a tremendous challenge has remained in the ability to network and integrate the individualized aspects of implementation while respectfully addressing each dynamic. These organizations have focused on the strategies for establishing or enhancing the ability to utilize data by exchange while respecting privacy concerns rooted in misinterpretations from bad exchanges (Marchibroda, 2004; HealthIT Dot Gov, 2014).

HL7

As user and infrastructure developmental competency requirements have increased along with the participation of state and federal regulatory organizations, the potential for society's realization of a safe and effective EHR system has grown. In addition to the aforementioned entities, clearly defining the rules of standardization for integration will go far in support of this potential. Health Level 7 International (HL7), which sets standards for clinical data exchanges, serves as an example of a prominent means to this end (Health Level 7 [HL7], 2014).

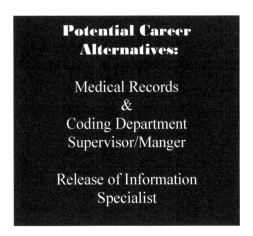

Potential Career Alternatives:

Medical Records
&
Coding Department
Supervisor/Manger

Release of Information
Specialist

Chapter Five ▲▼▲
Treatment Uses

Remote Medicine

"Jazz is a living organism...it's the cycles in nature and the music is bound to change into an organism that we might not even recognize. But you can't say that that's not Jazz, Jazz is just a word..."

● Matthew Shipp

Overview

It has been shown that for HIT strategies to become effective, a cultural shift from dysfunctional cookie-cutter production models towards efficient patient-centered treatment must become the systemic norm (Pronovost, et al., 2008). Remote medicine has provided professionally-guided treatment deliveries through HIT and informatics. By combining the real-time transfer of information, images, and CDS with providers in remote locations, the technology has increased access-to-care. Its application towards diagnostics and therapeutics has been proven through its use for critically ill patients aided by the elimination of risky transportation needs (Gackowski, et al., 2011). When combined with COE, remote medicine applications have proven to be useful enhancements to the continuum of care through provider-to-provider-to-patient exchanges with reduced medical error, i.e. allergies and contraindications (Kaushal, et al., 2006).

Teleconsultation

HIT remote consultative deliveries have shown to be achievable throughout health care. Just as other health care providers, I have benefited from the immediacy provided through electronically-aided health information exchanges (HIE) and digital images (Varkey, 2010). For those of us who've been equipped with this informatics tool, teleconsultation have been useful towards the standardized incorporation of images into EHR documentation, i.e. personal and medical, for better patient treatment. These processes have contributed to the achievement of IOM goals for enhanced evidence-based CDS during treatment (IOM, 2001). In addition to the immediacy provided through electronically-aided health information exchanges, the related digital images can be incorporated into the EHRs through standardized exchanges (Varkey, 2010). Among other various uses, i.e. case review and education, the technology's potential respecting increased patient safety has also been demonstrated through its ability to further reduce transportation needs for evaluations (Gackowski, et al., 2011).

Professional Education

Improved diagnostic and treatment case history with open disclosure through telemedicine has proved useful for oversight (Burton, 2009), organizational team liability assessments, and the development of ethical processes towards delivery (Galt & Paschal, 2011). It has remained a useful enhancement to the vital elements of medical and financial case study and peer review, i.e. providers, nurses, and administrators (Barr, 2010; Leatherman, et al., 2011).

Future implications continue to be exemplified through uses during the developmental processes of globally agreed upon standards, i.e. International Organization for Standardization (International Organization for Standardization [ISO], 2013), International Classification of Diseases (CDC, 2013), and the Joint Commission (JC, 2010), for useful common terminologies. Further, bio-intelligence and biomedical technology have supported academic and professional disciplines, i.e. medical and dental, by affording remote tele-surgery with virtual imagery and three-dimensional body scans (Tan, 2008).

Telemedicine

Telemedicine has supported health care cost reduction with increased patient safety through shared resources (Ward, Spragens, & Smithson, 2006). It has contributed to health care's developing infrastructure founded on useful exchanges and global integrations (Pronovost, et al., 2008). As exemplified through its use during pre and post-hospitalization (Bergrath, Rossaint, Lenssen, Fitzner, & Skorning, 2013), telemedicine has allowed for the modification of both emergency and chronic care deliveries for the better (Gackowski, et al., 2011). Telemedicine has been defined as remote treatment deliveries through informatics (Hebda & Czar, 2013). This technology also supports the IOM's goal of reduced disparity through increased access to *quality* care (IOM, 2001). This has been exemplified through usages for increased emergency medical service (EMS) and efficiency through the pre-hospital transmission of diagnostic images (Bergrath, Rossaint, Lenssen, Fitzner, & Skorning, 2013).

Telehealth

The WHO has defined telehealth as telemedicine used by providers other than the physician. These have included pharmacists, nurses, physical therapists, mental health professionals, and others (Hebda & Czar, 2013; Montague & Perchonok, 2012). Together with teleconsultation and telemedicine, all have remained applications of remote medicine for improved treatment access, delivery, and better outcomes.

Remote Dentistry

Prosthodontics

To demonstrate the potential respecting usages towards the aforementioned oral health crisis (Dye, Li, & Thornton-Evans, 2012; Slaughter & Evans, 2007), I will reference a study that was performed utilizing telemedicine for remote dentistry, in which video technology afforded the consultation of specialists from off-site locations. In an effort to address the provider shortages inherent to remote locations of India, the study focused on the potential for utilizing newly graduated dentists to provide on-site, technically-challenging care to patients in those areas. Care was delivered with the aid of tele-guided clinical support being provided by dental specialists. The research found the treatment to have been at the standard-of-care levels acceptable for that country. Further, results proved an increase in overall quality of care provided by all study groups through enhanced consultative efforts (Keeppanasseril, Matthew & Muddappa, 2011).

Treatment Uses

CAD/CAM

CAD/CAM technology (CAD/CAM) has also proved useful for dental providers (Poticny & Klim, 2010). By capturing three-dimensional patient images, the technology has allowed for the fabrication of prostheses through on-site computerized mills in treatment clinics that once required human fabrication within specialized laboratories (Poticny & Klim, 2010). This has allowed for a customized prosthesis to be fabricated with increased accuracy, and often in a single visit (DiMatteo, 2013).

CAD/CAM has allowed for the immediate and customized fabrication of surgical splints and abutments utilized during surgical implant placement or implant supported oral-maxillofacial reconstruction, by providing three-dimensional models based upon the bone densities and oral anatomy of a specific patient (Turkyilamz & Nicoll, 2010). As a result, generalized increases in a favorable treatment prognosis have been realized, and able to be delivered comprehensively at single locations (Patel, 2010). These delivery methods have increased the options and potentials for access-to-care respecting specialty procedures of remote locations. CAD/CAM has merged with other forms of biomedical technology (Tan, 2008). Specialized prostheses and procedures have grown to over 7 million restorations yearly with superior materials (Poticny & Klim, 2010). These uses, coupled with clinic transportability, have supported the view that the objectives for disparity reduction through remote dental informatics while maximizing access-to-care remain limitless (Dawkins, Michimi, Ellis-Griffith, Peterson, Carter, & English, 2013; IOM, 2001).

Health Information Exchanges

Defined through the Affordable Care Act (ACA), government policies have been geared for data collection standardization (Moskowitz, Guthrie, & Bindman, 2012). HIE approaches have attempted to address safety concerns through collaborative methods of evidence-based CDS (Bloomrosen & Detmer, 2010). The government has attempted to measure quality assurance and reward providers displaying evidence-based practices through standardized metrics (Goldsmith, 2011). The Healthcare Effectiveness Data and Information Set (HEDIS), has served as an example through a quasi financial pay-for-performance program (Moskowitz, Guthrie, & Bindman, 2012).

Many of us within health care have supported more research towards definitive conclusions respecting evidence-based pathways for the standardization of like-conditions and minimized service duplication. Respecting those concerns for an unfortunate disease trend common to African American communities, providers have reported the benefits of enhanced confidence through treatment option tools to include the identification and treatment of abusive or unwarranted drug patterns (Hincapie, Warholak, Murcko, Slack, & Malone, 2011). The potential for informatics-aided approaches towards pro-active strategies for treatment and prevention of drug abuse and other socially relevant diseases remains limitless.

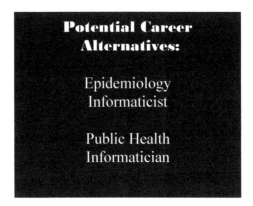

Potential Career Alternatives:

Epidemiology
Informaticist

Public Health
Informatician

Chapter Six ▲
Funding Better Medicine

"I think…Say, the way the economy is right now…the financial meltdown…when people think there is nothing, and we're going to loose everything. That's the time to get creative"

● Wayne Shorter

Overview

As mentioned earlier, the IOM called for the establishment of patient safety goals as part of a national agenda towards improving the US healthcare system respecting avoidable adverse events and deaths (IOM, 1999). That call for improved strategies of shared communication was identified within the 1999 IOM report called *To Err Is Human* (IOM, 1999). Funding for this task was recommended as a foreseeable objective for patient safety in the IOM's subsequent 2001 report called *Crossing the Quality Chasm* (IOM, 2001). Both reports supported the need for the US healthcare system to build a solid infrastructure for HIT systems (IOM, 2001).

In response, $19 billion was appropriated to spawn innovation and the useful applications of HIT and informatics in health information systems (HHS, 2009). The purpose of this milestone remains to improve treatment deliveries, medical communication, and patient safety practices under the six dimensions of quality identified through IOM (HHS, 2009; Wachter, 2010). The result of this funding respecting treatment uses has been the rapid implementation of aforementioned HIT and informatics, i.e. EHRs, CPOE/CEO, telemedicine, and the dedication of other electronic media for documentation, shared-communication, and information storage (Sittig, & Singh, 2012).

Cost Containment

Health care organizations have focused on developmental strategies for optimizing balances between quality assurance and efficiency of treatment deliveries for cost-control (Health Research Institute [HRI], 2014; Zelman, McCue, Glick, & Thomas, 2014). Traditional annual increases for US medical expenses were between 7 and 8 percent, and have currently stood at between 6 and 6.8 percent annually according to PwC's Health Research Institute (HRI, 2014). In general, the attention for us to remain focused on this dynamic has remained warranted for our nation to stay competitive in other markets. Following, examples have been drawn to HIT support-driven roles of cost containment approaches.

Quality

With specialized providers often hundreds of miles apart from each other, the landscape impacting the nation's overall access-to-care has remained an impactful contributor to rising costs. HIE and remote delivery systems have attempted to narrow the disparity gap through evidence-based support (Bloomrosen & Detmer, 2010). Health administrators and providers have acknowledged that more research is needed to draw definitive conclusions related to pathway commitment and anticipated cost reductions, i.e. standardization of like-conditions coupled with reduced service duplication.

Efficiency

A commonly agreed upon role for HIT towards cost reduction has been rooted in the promise of fulfilling key objectives for doing more with less, i.e. staff reduction and re-organization, making processes more efficient, and streamlined billing with reduced error or unpaid services (Payne et al., 2013). The promised contributions of HIT towards reducing the fall-out costs, i.e. legal liability and wasted medical resources, of duplicate or improper treatment have remained paramount to cost containment strategies (Arlotto, Birch, Crockett, & Irby, 2007). However, the reduction of lost revenues associated with improper billing or collections have remained just as vital to effective solutions of cost containment (Payne et al., 2013).

Payers

At this time, I think it is necessary to point out that other than realistic resolutions to disparity reductions, I have no political agenda. I am creative, not political, by nature which could explain some of the frustrations that I've encountered during my personal aims at community contribution. For me, having voted for President Obama proudly signaled the last *symbolic* hurdle to be conquered respecting an evidence-based African American achievement at the highest level.

But, as a community-vested stakeholder, the election of 2008 also meant it was time to get back to work. Not to in any way disrespect the electoral process. It is fundamentally needed. I just feel that over the course of our history, since the passage of civil rights legislation, there has remained enough hands-on to do long before arriving at the poles. Respecting the ACA, it remains a monumental achievement. For me, extending the access-to-care equates to the access-to-*shared responsibility* of improved health status levels for our nation, i.e. saving lives. Current trends respecting the recent outbreaks of influenza and enteroviruses (nationally) or the Ebola virus (globally) have again served to highlight the *exponential* impacts, i.e. containment and costs of potentially fatal health threat originations coupled with establishing pro-active preventive cultures of practice (Ohlheiser, 2014; Virology, 2014; WHO, n.d.). It's 8- million-plus, infinitely SQUARED. I think we should appreciate the good in what works, fix what's broke, and concentrate on collectively bettering our communities. That being said, and given the current nature of political climate related to the following topics, the following information has been provided to be absorbed objectively, and as I've witnessed it throughout my career as a minority health provider.

Prior to 1960, traditional health care deliveries were financially supported through fee-for-service, early combinations of Blue Cross Blue Shield (BCBS), and providers as the price-setters (Zelman, McCue, Glick, & Thomas, 2014). With the need to address coverage growth cost coupled with increases in an aging and non-working population (Moskowitz, Guthrie, & Bindman, 2012),

Medicare and pre-paid plans evolved as initial cost-containment strategies that have remained a central focus of US health reform since 1970 (Zelman, McCue, Glick, & Thomas, 2014).

Un-strapping national resources has required sensible attempts targeted at responsible containment (HRI, 2014). National and community level awareness respecting shared-risk and responsibility of our care delivery systems has grown to unprecedented levels (Barton, 2010; HRI, 2014), as global communication has become integrated into the daily cultures of current and future generations (Zelman, McCue, Glick, & Thomas, 2014). Further, informatics remains a vital aid to useful implementations and strategic re-organizations, as vested stakeholders continue to seek plans for obtaining optimum quality assurance levels balanced against financially-prudent deliveries. My friend, colleague and fellow HU alumnus, Dr. Rodney Bland of Franklin, VA, weighed on those concerns from his perspective, respecting the barriers associated with HIT adoption rates for medical professionals (personal communication January, 2015). As an independent podiatrist belonging to a smaller underserved community, he has become all too familiar with the challenges facing minority medical solo-practitioners:

The greatest barrier to independent/traditional practice is economical. As health care costs and business expenses increase disproportionate to actual reimbursements, there is a mathematical ceiling that is reached that is far lower than in a generation or two past. Incentives to computerize and modernize do not make up for the true cost of a practice. The actual art of practicing is no longer. Patient volume is the bottom line.

Following, focus has been drawn to roles played by employers, insurers, and government agencies coupled with the influences of HIT and informatics towards the future of health care payment systems and finance reform.

Employers

As the national costs associated with a fragmented and inefficient system have come to light, a continued focus for reforming the patchwork of public and private coverage models has remained (Barton, 2010; Oberlander, 2012; HRI, 2014). Paramount to the promise of reform success is the nation's acknowledgement that the burden remains collective, i.e. patients, employers, providers, payers, policy makers, and enforcers (HRI, 2014; Zelman, McCue, Glick, & Thomas, 2014). It has been proven that despite the government policies aimed at employers for increased access-to-care, many have remained uninsured for various reasons (Kaiser Commission on Medicaid and the Uninsured, 2014; Oberlander, 2012). With the passage of ACA, employers' focus must shift towards responsible initiatives of compliance while participating in meaningful solutions towards health care reform and in the collective interest of reaching optimal national health-status levels (HRI, 2014; Kaiser Commission on Medicaid and the Uninsured, 2014).

Insurers

An ongoing barrier to successful reform implementations has been the dismal past related to risk responsibility. Early evolutions of health care systems left the burden of risks on the insurer or payer (Zelman, McCue, Glick, & Thomas, 2014). As cost containment became a central focus of national reform, the provider risk-responsibility increased significantly as payers shifted to flat-rate or incentive based methods (HRI, 2014; Kaiser Commission on Medicaid and the Uninsured, 2014).

However, the result was often an increased quantitative output in highly concentrated populations coupled with decreased safety or quality assurance; as strategies lacked control over quality assurance oversight, and providers juggled ideal care options against fixed re-imbursement rates (Chernew, 2010). As a dental provider during the early 90's, I can attest to a major deficiency held by health management organizations (HMO) which unintentionally pitted fixed and capitated rate reimbursed dentists against the unregulated costs of laboratory and material suppliers (Chernew, 2010). That professional make-up pool consisted of many providers who were unattached to larger health organizations, i.e. self-contained specialized equipment or clinical delivery models. This dynamic was often coupled with individual material and overhead expenses known to have fluctuated between 55 and 70% for care provision.

As a result, I witnessed many providers having to choose between delivering evidence-based definitive care and stop-gap deliveries as a professional means for survival. This held true especially in low-income or underserved communities in which many patients could not even afford the pre-determined plan co-pays. Newer strategies such as Accountable Care Organizations (ACO), have attempted to achieve a shared responsibility through health plan and provider partnerships (Goldsmith, 2011). Bundled payment schemes aimed at shared-risks through episode-based and global payment models are supported by some health administrators for controlling price and quantity (Chernew, 2011). However, successful strategies will need to insure that all factors leading to patient care have been reflected appropriately to remove the mistrust that has developed from unsuccessful partnerships of the past (Nugent, 2010).

Government

Policy makers and health organizations alike have focused to find the appropriate balance between quality-of-care regulations and cost control in efforts to reduce long-term expense trends (HRI, 2014, Zelman, McCue, Glick, & Thomas, 2014). Regardless of the intent or rationale behind evidence-base pathways, data resources have proven only as effective as the policy, regulation, or legislation supporting its reformed applications (Moskowitz, Guthrie, & Bindman, 2012). Stakeholder leadership, i.e. health organizations, policy makers, employers, and enforcement (Borkowski, 2009), must remain astute at spearheading strategic collaborative initiatives aimed at establishing cost-efficient cultures for increased access to *safe* care (HRI, 2014; Studer, 2008).

Potential Career Alternatives:

Medical Records
&
Coding Department
Supervisor/Manager

Medical and Inpatient
Coders

Coding Auditors

Consumer Health
Informaticians

Clinical Analyst

Chapter Seven ▲▼▲
Informatics Systems Management

> "Making the simple complicated is commonplace; making the complicated simple, awesomely simple, that's creativity."
>
> ● Charles Mingus

Overview

As a whole, the systems architecture for information systems (IS) has been defined as a comprehensive application of the various resources and components of information technology (IT) to meet organizational needs through their communication, interaction, and cohesive integration (Tan & Payton, 2010). When applied to health care organizations, the architecture has represented the informational blueprint for strategic implementation towards the common objective of better treatment outcomes (Wagner, Lee, & Glasser, 2009). Focus will be drawn to the make-up and the influences impacting the architectural development of systems within health care organizations.

Interoperability

Interoperability is the term used by health and IT professionals to define the cohesive integration of informatics systems. Its purpose has been to generate data from one system to be understood in the same context by another (Dolin & Alschuler, 2011). Respecting the obvious concerns of privacy and legal issues, the greatest impediment to achieving system interoperability within and between health care organizations has been the lack of universal understanding, interpretation, and agreement for the meaning behind IT, informatics, and certification standards being governed by various bodies (Friedman, Schueth & Bell, 2009).

Based upon those standards, the need for a uniform level of competencies to be reached among those responsible for the architectural development and implementation of systems has remained, as true semantic interoperability or the major objective of HL7, continues to be established (Dolin & Alschuler, 2011). A financial burden has also proven inherent to health care systems practicing under such dysfunction (Stewart, Fernandes, Rodriguez-Huertas & Landzberg, 2010). Firm standards for universally accepted interoperability and certification requirements have been targeted to address this (Dolin & Alschuler, 2011).

Life Cycle

Components

Traditional cycles have been sectioned into staged parts. The first two stages are referred to as Systems Acquisition. The second and third stages are Implementation and Maintenance, respectively (Wagner, Lee, & Glasser, 2009). Just as the other aforementioned informatics initiatives, all of these parts are dictated by organizational prioritizations, complexity, and resources (Hersh & Wright, 2010; HHS, 2009).

Planning

Middle management and end-users, through diverse task-forces or teams, have usually been charged with the communication of goals as directed by the senior executives.

This process has drawn upon the experiences and needs of departmental representatives and providers to focus on the organizational strategy, independent of any proposed technology that may be used (Tan & Payton, 2010). Systems have been analyzed through various modeling techniques, i.e. data, process, and workflow (Hersh & Wright, 2010). This has allowed organizational leaders to wage the proposals for a new system acquisition against the possible inept applications of a current one for improvement (Wagner, Lee, & Glasser, 2009).

Project Management

As temporary endeavors, i.e. long and short, for delivering products that aid organizations to realize objectives, successful projects have demonstrated the appropriate combination of individual skill-sets, methodical strategies, and resources (Project Management Institute, Inc. [PMI], 2013). Project planning for clearly defined deliverables, or scope (Ward, n.d.), communicated through project proposals, i.e. services and IT implementations in support of ongoing programs (Glaser, 2009); have aimed to satisfy these demands (Project Management Institute, Inc., 2013).

Project managers, teams, and workgroups have all represented elements of influence towards successful projects of programs aligned with organizational culture, mission, and vision (Meredith, Shafer, Mantel, & Sutton, 2014). Project management methodology has benefited organizations by providing a strategic tool for aligning various project tasks, i.e.

organizationally and inter-departmentally, through evidence-based practice selections (Meredith, Shafer, Mantel, & Sutton, 2014).

The level of categorization with respect to project scope provided through these methods (Wyllie, 2004), has facilitated the successful tailoring of IT support products to meet end-user demands while assuring the inter-departmental interoperability required for seamless integrations throughout organizations (Hebda & Czar, 2013). This has resulted in organizational portfolios comprised of interrelated project management schemes aimed at furthering the overall mission of the organization and its common stakeholders (Meredith, Shafer, Mantel, & Sutton, 2014). However, none of the aforementioned efforts have proven traditionally successful without proper planning (Hefner & Malcolm, 2002). The remaining focus will be drawn to the contrasting comparisons of strategic and tactical planning levels coupled with useful IT in support of project management methods.

Strategic

Strategic planning has aimed to reflect the long-term mission objectives of organizational executives and senior stakeholders (Englebardt & Nelson, 2002). As the resulting product of management's assessment for risks, organizational deficiencies, and capacity balanced against goals, it is communicated top down as a tool for planning objectives to be based. Early involvement with effective and on-going communication between project managers and those with the authority to approve or discontinue project resources, i.e. processes, funding, and equipment, have proven vital to project success. Successful models have continued to incorporate an IS application portfolio, i.e. administrative, financial, clinical and decision support, as organizational aids for strategic planning (Englebardt & Nelson, 2002; Hebda & Czar, 2013).

Tactical

Tactical plans have been defined by the set parameters of senior management through the organization's strategic plan. In response, project groups of managers, teams, and end-users have served to develop methods for delivering the results (Glaser, 2009). Successful plans have incorporated all impacted stakeholders. Communication to executives has often been supported through informatics. Often aided by automated IT tools, i.e. progress reports and earned value assessment (EVA) applications, managers have used tactical plans as dynamic and definitive backbones for managing scope, prioritizations, member roles, and milestones of projects (Englebardt & Nelson, 2002; Hefner & Malcolm, 2002).

All levels of planning and stakeholders have proven vital to successful projects and the implementation of on-going programs (Kropf & Scalzi, 2008). Given the history of interdisciplinary fragmentation, i.e. multi-providers, specialists and payers, that have traditionally plagued health care delivery systems, portfolios of effective project management (PM) solutions aimed at furthering the overall mission of organizations and their common stakeholders have remained vital to the success of isolated organizational projects (PMI, 2013). Effective PM methodologies have contributed to repositories of evidence-based practice management strategies to be utilized throughout all of health care.

Design

At this phase, task-force teams have traditionally been coupled with data analysts; financial and project managers; and informational technology representatives, i.e. internal or external. System needs have been clearly defined and evaluated through a cost-benefit analysis (Wagner, Lee, & Glasser, 2009). Resources through the Information Technology Infrastructure Library (ITIL) have often been incorporated (Hildreth, 2007). Resources to be considered have included staff certification for evidence-based management, and IT schemes (Information Technology Infrastructure Library [ITIL], 2013).

Potential Career Alternatives:

Computer Systems Engineer

HIT Implementation Project Manager

IS Quality Assurance Tester

Chapter Eight ▲▼▲

IS Finance, Implementation & Maintenance

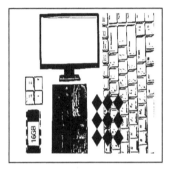

Adam's ARTHouse©

"Two or three times a year I ask the students to write me a letter criticizing or making complaints or suggestions about anything connected with the institution. When this is not done, I have them meet me in the chapel for a heart-to-heart talk about the conduct of the school."

● Booker T. Washington

Overview

In his 1901 autobiography *Up from Slavery* (Washington, 2013), Booker T. Washington was discussing feedback concerning the finance, implementation, and maintenance of Tuskegee Institute, now University, as its establishing principal. Respecting efforts towards the effective prioritization of those objectives, he further explained, "There are no meetings with our students that I enjoy more than these, and none are more helpful to me in planning for the future." For organizational investments in HIT applications and implementations, though often mandated through the global and national enforcement of governmental standardization (Lang, 2014), the measures for evaluating returns on investment (RIO) have remained two-fold (HRI, 2014). Implementations for patient safety and cost-reduction have had to consider the *actual* gains against potentials for unwanted technology-induced errors and their related infrastructure fixes (Borycki, Kushniruk, & Carvalho, 2013). Analytical dilemmas have been rooted in waging *tangible* versus *non-tangible* gains (Eskelin, 2001; Parente & Van Horn, 2006), during the appropriate coupling of revenue producers with cost-centers towards organizational goals and missions (Zelman, McCue, Glick, & Thomas, 2014).

Proven evidence-based returns from capital investments such as operating room expansions have been embedded within overall strategic-growth plans that have reflected visions for organizational sustainability through the cyclic renewal of patient safety, satisfaction, and increased health outcome initiatives (Eskelin, 2001; Barton, 2010). Regardless of the anticipated return type, successful evaluations have struck the proper balance of risk versus reward (Bassi, & Lau, 2013). They have proportionally reflected potential gains, i.e. increased risks equals increased rewards (Zelman, McCue, Glick, & Thomas, 2014), within chosen investment strategies (Arlotto, Birch, Crockett, & Irby, 2007). Following are common methods and considerations practiced by health care organizations towards the evaluation of HIT investment returns.

Successful implementations of HIT solutions have coupled the prioritized dedication of organizational resources, i.e. evaluation, selection, and purchase, with appropriate strategies for long-term usage, maintenance, and support (Eskelin, 2001; Glaser, 2006). The optimum balance between quality assurance and efficiency of treatment deliveries afforded through successful solutions has remained reliant on the accurate forecasting of background expenses, i.e. training, end-user promotion, and system recovery (Hersh & Wright, 2010; HRI, 2014), and resulted in long-term benefits for safety and financial stability (Zelman, McCue, Glick, & Thomas, 2014). Focus will be drawn to business and financial considerations for sustained HIT adoption, support, maintenance, and stability.

Financial

With analytical results having often proved type specific, i.e. primary care, COE, and CDS (Bassi, & Lau, 2013), methods for evaluating the potential for tangible or revenue-generating returns has remained defined through bottom-line approaches geared towards organizational dollar value (Aggelidis & Chatzoglou, 2008). Cost and impact data has often been retrieved from like-organizations to generate target metrics through cost-benefit analysis (CBA), cost-consequence analysis (CCA), and cost effectiveness analysis (CEA) for similar strategic investments based on benefits, effectiveness, and savings (Bassi, & Lau, 2013).

Concepts such as Net Present Value (NPV), i.e. direct input cost over time (Zelman, McCue, Glick, & Thomas, 2014), have been compared to projected revenue gains obtained through linear or logistic regression statistical estimations for financial feasibility assessments (Bassi, & Lau, 2013). The methods for deriving the NPV account for the time value of money by allowing managers to wage cost investment against realistic ways for funding the proposed investment over time (Arlotto, Birch, Crockett, & Irby, 2007). Consistent with the aforementioned theoretical metrics of cost and impact, marginal analysis have also been used successfully to explore the incremental effects on revenue returns associated with minimal input or output product alternatives.

Operation and Management
Financial

Unforeseen risks such as future governance, economy, and market shifts have remained inherent cost impacts and barriers to the accurate forecasting by administrators and financial executives (MacTaggart, & Hyatt Thorpe, 2013). Successful schemes have displayed an appreciation for these vital factors (Arlotto, Birch, Crockett, & Irby, 2007; HRI, 2014), while reflecting the comprehensive understanding of the *actual* costs expenses associated with successful implementations, i.e. research, evaluation, team development, and resource allocation. Organizations have sought to align external policy-based initiatives with internal goals for financing the development and/or establishment of the infrastructure required from meaningful use implementations (HHS, 2009; MacTaggart, & Hyatt Thorpe, 2013).

Not to be ignored, training for tasked implementers and end-users, test-pilot unit resources, long-term support, maintenance and system up-dating have remained key cost considerations (Eskelin, 2001; Hersh & Wright, 2010; HHS, 2009). Having considered the aforementioned factors, the active engagement of the organization's project sponsor has remained vital to successful finance negotiations and for creative funding strategies (Eskelin, 2001). Organizational strategies have included the proper training, allocation, and funding of internal resources such as super-users, coupled with external resource options, i.e. off-site data securities, for long-term stability and protection.

Non-financial

Intangible gains have been defined through internal origins such as clinical impact and user application rates (Aggelidis & Chatzoglou, 2008). External impacts such as competitiveness, good-will, and governmental compliance towards safety have remained at the heart of non-financial revenues (Zelman, McCue, Glick, & Thomas, 2014). The SMArt platform has been applied to the comprehensive evaluation of social, financial, political capital impact of investment for HIT. The method has been used to insure that factors for optimality, contingency, and usefulness have been appropriately considered during the evaluation of organizational investment returns (Ramly & Flatley Brennan, 2012).

As organizational value has remained a matter of interpretation defined through missions and goals (Eskelin, 2001; Parente & Van Horn, 2006), methods embedded within frameworks such as the Performance of Routine Information System Management (PRISM) have proved useful as tools for evaluating HIT on system performance (Aquil, Lippeveld, & Hozumi, 2009). Ongoing monitoring has been identified as key to the accurate assessment of tangible and non-tangible impacts (Aggelidis & Chatzoglou, 2008). Increased organizational value tied to marketable attributes afforded through better health outcomes (Eskelin, 2001; HRI, 2014), and produced from the cyclic improvement of process inputs and outputs has remained (Aquil, Lippeveld, & Hozumi, 2009).

Operation and Management
Non-financial

The ever-changing, often non-repeatable, or type specific dynamics of health care culture, i.e. patient, departmental, and organizational, have proven barriers to be overcome during the development of successful HIT resolutions (Kotter, 2007). Successful investments have remained hinged on the adoption of technology within cultural processes coupled with the usage rates of vested stakeholders that have been convinced of the proposed ultimate return on investments (Arlotto, Birch, Crockett, & Irby, 2007), represented as organizational value, CDS, and ease of adherence to governmental compliance (Payne et al., 2013).

Evidence-based comparatives delivered through the research of health administrators, project teams, and engaged providers as ultimate ground-floor end-users (McClellan, Casalino, Shortell, & Rittenhouse, 2013), have assisted in deriving predictions for the anticipated quantitative and qualitative cost to be considered. Clearly defined organizational objectives for efficiency and safety have often proven to be obtained through a reworking of faulty human-processes, as opposed to technology driven solutions, through evidence-based evaluation processes. These approaches have remained critical to prioritizations, i.e. risk aversion (Arlotto, Birch, Crockett, & Irby, 2007), and product selection as successes have been heavily based on end-user commitments rooted in enhanced confidence and support measures for treatment delivery schemes (Pevnick et al., 2012).

Other factors have shown to be related to the accurate assessment(s) of an organization's internal pre-implementation resources, i.e. onboard hardware capacities and interoperability (Arlotto, Birch, Crockett, & Irby, 2007), waged against external options, i.e. outsourcing and data reserves (Johnson, Murphy, McNeese, Reddy, & Purao, 2013). Post-implementation factors have included operational considerations, i.e. change request, fixes, and enhancements (Eskelin, 2001), coupled with realistic schemes for addressing disaster, data-breaches (Pevnick et al., 2012), or complete system failure.

The influential factors towards the prudent financial decisions and strategic plans of health care organizations have remained a fluctuating dynamic (Zelman, McCue, Glick, & Thomas, 2014). Methods for financial evaluation have remained true to key components, i.e. perspective, comparative options, costs, and outcomes (Bassi, & Lau, 2013). Comprehensive evaluations of intangible benefits, i.e. increased access-to-care, resource allocation and safety, have continued to drive research towards evidence based solutions (Aggelidis & Chatzoglou, 2008). Though expressed ROI successes have not always been through bottom-line derivatives, all have remained bound to sound economic evaluations when considering the tangible and intangible benefits of proposed HIT investments (Bassi, & Lau, 2013; HRI, 2014).

Sustainability

The financial stability of health care organizations has remained an indispensible concern of impact with respect to the dynamics of reliable care, i.e. long and short term delivery (Zelman, McCue, Glick, & Thomas, 2014). Through ratio analysis, proper assessments have proven equally important for provider retention and recruitment, comprehensive care scheme development, and vendor partnerships while seeking, producing, and maintaining evidence-based performance levels supported through HIT. The traditional negative *net*-incomes of some organizations have proven detrimental to successful parings through the increased shared-risks of individual organizational investments towards common objectives (Eskelin, 2001; HRI, 2014). Focus will be drawn to the importance for the proper assessment of balance sheets, income, and cash flow statements through ratio analysis tools as useful resources towards the appropriate evaluation of financial sustainability in health care organizations.

Balance Sheet

As an organizational summary of assets, liabilities, and equity (U.S. National Library of Medicine [NIH/NLM], 2014), balance sheets have been used to evaluate its positive resources waged against its negatives for financial health assessments. Sheet derivatives have been defined as net assets (U.S. Securities and Exchange Commission [SEC], 2014; Zelman, McCue, Glick, & Thomas, 2014). It has remained a snap-shot evaluation tool for analyzing an organization's financial health status through stakeholder equity (HIH/NLM, 2014), and at a given point-in-time (SEC, 2014; Zelman, McCue, Glick, & Thomas, 2014).

Income Statement

Revenues garnered during the regular operations waged against the expenses used to generate them are represented within the income statement (SEC, 2014). It has remained important for income statements to be combined with other ratio tools for comparison to achieve a comprehensive understanding of financial statuses, i.e. trend analysis towards profitability and solvency (Lane, Longstreth, & Nixon, 2001). The *net*-income identified through income statements has been used by health organizations to identify resources for operation improvements and cash reserve generation (SEC, 2014).

Cash Flow

As the ultimate measure of its ability to respond to uncontrollable forces, i.e. governmental policy, provider fluctuation, and like-market competitive forces, the statement of cash flows has remained the best indicator of an organization's financial health (SEC, 2014; Sussman, Grube, & Samaris, 2009). The statement has been used to explain how revenues were generated and the associated cost to resources (SEC, 2014; Zelman, McCue, Glick, & Thomas,

2014). Common ratios used for its measurement include operating margin ratio, days-in-accounts-receivable (AR) ratio, current ratios, and capital ratios (SEC, 2014). By analyzing how organizational assets have been financed compared with its ability to negotiate additional debt, capital structure ratios have been used to evaluate cash-flow health (SEC, 2014; Zelman, McCue, Glick, & Thomas, 2014).

A primary goal of health organizations has been to create financial schemes that optimize the level of cash-on-hand afforded to mitigate socio-economic fluxes (Sussman, Grube, & Samaris, 2009). Proper analysis achieved through using the statement of cash flows has given organizations the ability to un-mask revenue deficiencies hidden within income statements by considering the re-imbursement times, i.e. delays of products and services (SEC, 2014), related to external health care dynamics (Panel on Measuring Medical Care Risk in Conjunction with the New Supplemental Income Poverty Measure, 2007).

All financial evaluation tools have remained vital to accurate assessments of health organizational viability and sustainability (SEC, 2014; Zelman, McCue, Glick, & Thomas, 2014). Such assessments have served to insure that managed expenses have reflected financial strategic plans with returns having met or exceeded bench-marked expectations (Sussman, Grube, & Samaris, 2009). Strong evaluation methods for determining the long-term stability of potential partners have proven essential for achieving on-going research and development, sustainable clinical decision and technological support, and the adaptability for policy-imposed standardization maintenance with respect to tech-savvy health organizations (Needleman, 2003).

Successful organizations have developed cultures of monthly profit-lost statement evaluation practices towards pro-active measures for sustainability (Lane, Longstreth, & Nixon, 2001). Overhead expenses and resource costs are waged against patient care disciplines to reach conclusive ends (NIH/NLM, 2014; SEC, 2014). Through horizontal and vertical analysis (Zelman, McCue, Glick, & Thomas, 2014), cyclic re-assessments towards optimal financial performance have proven useful in uncovering organizational trends, i.e. positive and negative, and setting precedence for the establishment of long-term financial cultures (SEC, 2014; Zelman, McCue, Glick, & Thomas, 2014).

Implementation

Insufficient attention to all aspects of the cost and investment of HIT implementations have proven to have severe consequences, i.e. stalled implementations, wasted or unrecoverable financial investment, and/or ongoing costly down-times (SEC, 2014). Responsible organizational strategies for successfully schemed implementations have proven to reflect the proper balance of financial and non-financial considerations for long-term support, operation, and cultural adoption (SEC, 2014; Eskelin, 2001). They have also remained properly budgeted within the comprehensive financial management strategies characteristic to sustainable organizations (Zelman, McCue, Glick, & Thomas, 2014).

At the implementation stage, resources have also been allocated for installation, testing, data conversions, and staff preparations for the system to *go-live*. (Wagner, Lee, & Glasser, 2009). It is often been aided by ITIL resources which have been accessed by internal IT professionals, departmental managers, and end-users (AXELOS, 2014; McLaughlin, 2005). Training, implementation, and management schemes have all been made available through the ITIL (ITIL, 2013b).

Maintenance

Feedback, often delivered through the departmental *rounding* of end-users, has been utilized by IT representatives for analysis and support maintenance (Eskelin, 2001). Resources have been dedicated towards keeping mission-critical systems functional 99.99% of the time, to include personnel, infrastructure, technological developments, and upgrades. Dialogue between system financial managers has remained paramount as this phase, and has often accounted for 80% of the information system budget (Eskelin, 2001; Wager, Lee, & Glasser, 2009). The most effective implementations have involved prioritized one-step-at-a-time approaches. The dialogue between high, mid, and low level users has proven vital to remain current respecting IT developments, which may impact or influence various applications of the system development life cycle (SDLC) for sustainability (Eskelin, 2001; Tan & Payton, 2010).

Chapter Nine ▲▼▲
Architecture & Infrastructure

> "The greatest people that we admire today
> they, they did more than that, they just, they
> were more than just great players or great
> technicians or you know great stylists, they,
> the great ones really had the vision…"
>
> ● Ravi Coltrane

Overview

Systems architecture has included all of the components for IT infrastructure as well as the providers, administrators, and governance that contribute to its general make-up and implementation (Arraj, 2013). Systems infrastructure has been primarily represented by the organization's computers, networks, and their associated applications or platforms. Sound characteristics of effective systems architecture have proven to reflect in the quality of organizational leadership coupled with the relationship between IT and health organizations (Van Sante & Ermers, 2009; Vicente, 2013; Wager, Lee, & Glasser, 2009).

With respect to those qualities and to software investments traditionally accounting for 75% of the computer-systemic cost, health care organizational principles and philosophies have coupled with applicable levels of standardization, to lend long-term sustainability and global relevance to the architecture (AXELOS, 2014; Tan & Payton, 2010). To serve as examples, Microsoft and Cisco have existed as platforms common to the standardized practices of health care systems due to wide-spread usage (Cisco, 2014; Microsoft, 2014; Wager, Lee, & Glasser, 2009). This philosophy has remained in-line with the long-term-agenda of the American Health Information Management Association, or AHIMA (Dougherty, 2006). It was reflected in their Statement of Data Stewardship of 2008 (American Health Information Management Association [AHIMA], 2007). Various approaches to systems architecture have been applied and have included the client-to-server approach and the application-to-service provider approach, among others, in which data has been hosted remotely (Wager, Lee, & Glasser, 2009; Van Sante & Ermers, 2009; Vicente, 2013).

Windows NT

This architectural approach has used a database layer, dictated by messaging standards, and combined with application, authentication, and authorization layers (Held, n.d.; Vogels, 1999). Semantics standards have provided interoperability between the repositories or layers, and allowed for entries performed in one layer to appear in others as needed during treatment deliveries (Held, n.d.; Vogels, 1999).

SOA

Service-oriented architecture (SOA), with service-oriented computing (SOC), has met the expanded demands of a globalized modern economy coupled with its inherent organizational diversities (Tosic, 2010). Its software components have been accessed for re-use or extended for increased interoperability (Monegain, 2007). However, its potential has been hampered by system unpredictability (Panahi, Nie, & Lin, 2010).

Data versus Information

Music is a world within itself;
with a language we all understand
— Stevie Wonder

Improved provider connectivity, treatment deliveries, health status levels and provider-to-facility alignment with technological interoperability have resulted in the quest for strategies for obtaining data for informational applications within health care organizations (Tan & Payton, 2010). Data management must merge the philosophical goals, staff functions, and treatment delivery needs with the safety and standard-of-care protocols of providers. Heath management information systems (HMIS), have defined knowledge, network, system, interoperability and management as structural components (HIMSS Health Information Exchange Steering Committee, 2009; Tan & Payton, 2010). Heath care data frameworks of patient encounters include *patient specific*, *aggregate* and *comparative* as subcategories (Wager, Lee, & Glasser, 2009). Focus will be drawn to the relationship of obtaining useful data and strategies of informational development to gain knowledge or wisdom.

Data represents the atomic elements obtained, and correlated into informational streams, to interpret a particular patient's condition or health status. The interpretation of informational data is influenced by individual biases, expertise and agendas. Therefore, effective HMIS planning strategies should be continuous, adaptable, and respectful of all stakeholders (HIMSS Health Information Exchange Steering Committee, 2009; Tan & Payton, 2010). With guidance through organizations such as the AHIMA (AHIMA, 2008), sustainable HMIS is built upon a shared architectural foundation of defined data-to-information towards gaining the desired knowledge and wisdom (Kaipa, 2000).

As the primary elements of communication, data always represent symbols out of context (Kaipa, 2000). Quality data is completely understandable, serves its purposeful intent upon retrieval and is re-usable by other disciplines. Its quality is directly tied to life-and-death risk treatment outcomes (Amatayakul, 2008; HIMSS Health Information Exchange Steering Committee, 2009). This was supported by the Long-term Care's Industry Summit of 2005 through its declaration of intent to become advocates for adopting data content and messaging standards of cross-care interoperability (Doughery, 2006). As participants, AHIMA standards were established (AHIMA, 2007). As repositories, data bases are characteristically specific. Relational data bases, which target financial or administrative tasks, allow for one-to-one, one-to-many, many-to-one or many-to-many relationships between data entities (Tan & Payton, 2010). Object-oriented data bases with the ability to tie images to body parts are often coupled with other specialized data bases to provide hybridized HMIS focused on comprehensive deliveries (HIMSS Health Information Exchange Steering Committee, 2009).

As processed or structured data, information represents the defined contextual relationship of data (Kaipa, 2000). An example of applied context to data symbols to yield information is represented by common blood pressure readings. In addition to its useful original intent, quality data is often mined, i.e. data mining, to disclose useful health status trends to aid in disease or accident prevention and treatment efficiency (Wager, Lee, & Glaser, 2009).

Standardization

"What makes each great musician great is how they interpret or how they process the information that they're given." — Jason Moran

Technical standards have served as guidelines, based upon widely accepted definitions, to allow for the proper and meaningful transfer of data (Englebart & Nelson, 2002). Interoperability has been aided by coordinating agencies that have insured the required level of applicable guidelines has been met (Hebda & Czar, 2013). A universal understanding, interpretation, and agreement of coordinated technical standards by user organizations has been required to solidify the architectural foundation upon which effective strategic implementations of health care informatics systems can be rooted (Friedman, Schueth & Bell, 2009).

Identifier, general communications, and specific communications have represented technical standards. Identifier standards have applied to electronic patient specification. General communications standards have been aimed at electronic message communication. Specific communication standards have defined imaging and other informational exchanges within health care (Englebart & Nelson, 2002). On the following pages, focus has been drawn to patient identifiers, HL7, digital imaging, and communications respecting their associated coordinating organizations.

Development

Many organizations have adopted internal and external reporting methods in response to the international focus on quality assurance, safety, and access-to-care. In response, the IOM called for the increased utilization of HIT to aid in national and international standardization coupled with sound infrastructures based upon evidence-based strategies for development (IOM, 2001; ITIL, 2013b). These are needed to assure the accuracy of data to be compiled, studied, and shared globally (AHIMA, 2007).

Standardized reporting for, and between, the CMS and other health organizations remains a vital aid to successful efforts of raising health status levels and achieving the optimum efficiency sought for health care delivery systems (Barton, 2010; Moskowitz, Guthrie, & Bindman, 2012).

Focus will be drawn to the value of supplementing the core measurement processes of CMS standards with ISO standardization for the global interoperability of exchanges between systems and the accumulation of data for research and improvements (Hebda & Czar, 2013; ISO, 2013).

CMS

The Centers for Medicaid & Medicare Services has established processes for the reporting of quality assurance and safety data through core measurements, i.e. inspection, timeliness of care, outcomes, and patient satisfaction (HHS, n.d.). The results are made available to and from the public domain and to other organizations of safety and quality assurance, i.e. JC, HCAHPS, and the CDC (HHS, n.d.). The data collected and shared through these processes may be utilized by all stakeholders to explore treatment delivery options, make organizational assessments, and fuel health data repositories (HHS, n.d.).

ISO

Considering the IOM's objective of shared data for research, as a generalized framework for the international standardization of data exchanges, the International Organization for Standardization (ISO) has proved a useful supplement to CMS standards (IOM, 2001; Varkey, 2010). The limitations of ISO standardization towards clinical research data have been identified as being too broad when compared to others that have been primed for this, i.e. ICD-9, ICD-10, and SNOMED CT (Richesson & Nadkarni, 2011). However, the value of ISO supplementation to CMS standards is in its ability to standardize the general processes and equipment expectations for acquiring information and treatment deliveries, i.e. vendors and end-users (ISO, 2013).

The ISO is the largest developer, publisher, and organizational network of international standards (ISO, 2013). Its aim is to improve the global applications of quality assurance with improved efficiency through common terminologies (Varkey, 2010). The ISO has established a wide range of useful health care standards, i.e. aseptic processing and sterilization, medical equipment development, health informatics, and coding (ISO, 2013). Through a process of global consensus in response to market-need (ISO, 2013), the ISO remains uniquely positioned to define quality improvements through internationally accepted standard-of-care practices (Varkey, 2010).

The need for a solid HIT infrastructure has been identified by the IOM. The usefulness for data exchanges towards improved health status levels has proven vital to quality assessment measures. A global focus has been directed towards agreed upon standards for informatics to improve interoperability between systems (Hebda & Czar, 2013; IOM, 2001; ISO, 2013). The need for organizations to be proactive in processes for up-to-date reporting and responding to deficiencies with urgency has also been established. ISO standardization helps to assure the accuracy and international usefulness of medical data collection (ISO, 2013). This supports the IOM recommendation of utilizing technology for feedback, data collection, and as resources for evidence-based practices (IOM, 2001). It also allows health care organizations to learn and adapt through experiences exemplified on a global level (ISO, 2013). Standardized data and report forms can reduce the study process while increasing the facilitation of data sharing (Richesson & Nadkarni, 2011).

ISO compliance remains a voluntary global initiative. Participation and governance is proportional to the vested interest of health care stakeholders, i.e. nationally and globally, in quality assurance and patient safety improvements (ISO, 2013). As a multi-disciplined organizational classifier, participation is not intended as a replacement for more specified levels of medical standardization, i.e. JC and CMS (ISO, 2013; Varkey, 2010). ISO standards have proven useful in attempts to standardize data element repositories, i.e. National Cancer Institute and Clinical Data Interchange Standards Consortium (Richesson & Nadkarni, 2011). However, due to its broad scope, its usefulness respecting clinical research data has remained limited. The value of ISO membership remains its proven ability to serve as a framework for globally accepted quality improvement strategies (ISO, 2013; Richesson & Nadkarni, 2011).

Patient Data

CMS measurements include processes for patient access to quality measures and post-treatment feedback, i.e. patient survey and treatment claim data (HHS, n.d.). The ISO also contains specified standards for related data, i.e. gateway for home electronic systems, patient health care data, and information security (IOM, 2001). Standardized patient information made useful internationally supports the IOM's objective of improvements through evidence-based practices (HHS, n.d.; IOM, 2001).

Suppliers

CMS standards for structural measurements are utilized by health care vendors. Healthcare-associated infections, i.e. equipment and process related, also contribute to the data (HHS, n.d.) The suppliers of health care delivery systems for research and treatment, i.e. equipment and informatics, are achieved through global exchanges of free-market enterprises (Barton, 2010). These exchanges include onsite and remote deliveries of treatment and resources, i.e. telemedicine, distanced based manufacturers, and suppliers (Hebda & Czar, 2013). The ISO has established standards for the information to be useful to all of these aforementioned stakeholders as a global resource (ISO, 2013).

The CMS standards and core measurements have proven to be a useful resource for patient-centered care, quality, and safety improvement (HHS, n.d.). However, if the objectives identified by the IOM through its recommendations are to be realized (IOM, 2001), strategies for the proper comparisons of evidence-based improvements to health care systems needs to based upon research obtained through globally-useful data (Giannangelo, 2010). ISO supplementation supports these efforts by serving as a universal framework from which to build upon the common interest of national and international stakeholders for the overall improvement of health care delivery systems, treatment outcomes, and health status levels (ISO, 2013).

Patient Identifiers

Patient identifiers have reduced the amount of patient number accumulation. VirginiaCORIS, an application within correctional facilities, serves as a primary example by merging all of the personal, provider and institutional numbers previously assigned to the inmates with a single patient identifier to be utilized universally throughout the system (National Association of State Chief Information Officers [NASCIO], 2012).

HIPAA
Data

In addition to privacy, HIPAA has functioned to improve efficiency in the management of health care. With respect to patient identifier standardization, the primary objectives of HIPAA have been to reduce the duplication of documentation, while securing and maintaining patient privacy (Pike, 2009).

HL7

As an international standards-setting organization, it has developed messaging format protocols for the communication of various health care applications between each other (Dolin, 2010). An effective example has been its ability to reduce patient admittance times. Its Application Protocol for Electronic Data Exchange in Healthcare Environments has allowed patient accounts to be triggered and generated upon admittance for utilization by all necessary departments. HL7 has been coordinated through the ANSI Healthcare Informatics Standards Board (ANSI HISB) committee (Englebart & Nelson, 2002).

DICOM

Digital Imaging and Communications in Medicine (DICOM) was developed by the American College of Radiology and the National Electrical Manufacturer's Association (NEMA). They set the standard for diagnostic and therapeutic image exchanges (Englebart & Nelson, 2002). Establishment and implementation of these standards has allowed for the widespread utilization in clinical applications of imaging technology throughout medicine (Thomas, 2008).

Potential Career Alternatives:

Analytic Reporting
Developer

Clinical/Sustainability
Analyst

Clinical Data
Analyst

Clinical Informatics
Coordinator

IT Clinical
Analyst

Medical Informatics
Researcher

Meditech Clinical
Analyst

Chapter Ten ▲▼▲

Organizational Needs

> "We [scientists] have often striven to prove life as wholly mechanistic, starting with the hypothesis that organisms are machines! Living substance is such because it possesses this organization--something more than the sum of its minutest parts."
>
> ● Ernest E. Just

Overview

Known as the Black Apollo of Science (Manning, 1983), Dr. Just was referring to cell biology. However, his words remain respectfully symbolic of the organizational dynamics concerning institutions. Health organizations are communities within themselves. In a microcosmic view, they are the collective grouping of leaders, developers, strategists, educators, and consumers. And just as it is true for racially or ethnically identifiable communities, i.e. family and social, they are charged daily with addressing their human, equipment, and economic resource needs to sustain them. The following pages have drawn focus to those evidence-based concerns to be addressed for successful implementations of informatics.

Health Organizations

Parameters for quantified staffing ratios, roles, educational and leadership pre-requisites, and competencies have yet to be defined (Hersh, 2010). However, the need for a culturally and technologically diverse workforce has been established (Borkowski, 2009; Hersh, 2010). The IOM has defined informatics as an essential core competency towards patient-centered care (Hersh, 2010). From a technical aspect, successful implementations have included evidence-based definitions for infrastructure with respect to networking and computational resources (Hersh, 2010). The evidence has also demonstrated that a comprehensive knowledge of finance, acquisition, and resource appropriation respecting clinically specific applications has remained for meaningful uses (Buchbinder & Shanks, 2012; Hersh, 2010).

Fig 10.1

It has been shown that for culturally building a cyclic framework, future educational and career models must reflect the needs specific to defined workforce roles such as collecting patient data, analytical research, and clinical application (Hersh, 2010; Bloomrosen & Detmer, 2010; Buchbinder & Shanks, 2012). As demonstrated in Figure 10.1, successful models have remained an amalgamation of basic, translational, and clinical research efforts (Bloomrosen & Detmer, 2010). As a result, potential career-paths have included; health information technology management, project management, clinical informatics professionals, biomedical informatics (BMI), and clinical and translational science, or CTS (Hersh, 2010; Payne, Pressler, Sarkar, & Lussier, 2011).

It has been argued that the aim should be for the provision of realistic health care career alternatives, and framed in the interest of early stakeholder investment towards global solutions (Hersh, 2010). Through the collaborative efforts of organizational stakeholders, such as the American Medical Informatics Association (AMIA) and the AHIMA, attempts to define related educational pre-requites and competencies have been made. The results have led to the inclusion of over 118 million dollars of allocated funding within governmental initiatives specific to workforce development. These have included curriculum development and competency certification, coupled with grants afforded to university programs, i.e. graduate certificates and master's degree levels (Hersh, 2010).

Assessment

Strategies have called for the identification of insufficient community resource pools to be targeted through leadership (Johnson, Murphy, McNeese, Reddy & Purao, 2013). Successful models have insured that organizations remained cognizant of leadership versus managerial ratios (Buchbinder & Shanks, 2012). It has also been shown that health care disparity and various proposed HIT solutions towards resource needs, workforce development, and implementation, have remained common to rural and urban communities (Buchbinder & Shanks, 2012; Johnson, Murphy, McNeese, Reddy & Purao, 2013). Both have called for innovative methods to address the associated financial and human resource shortages (Johnson, Murphy, McNeese, Reddy & Purao, 2013).

Many larger facilities have addressed the majority of their IT needs in-house. Smaller urban facilities have often opted to outsource needful resources (Johnson, Murphy, McNeese, Reddy & Purao, 2013). Though this has boded well for addressing resource-ratios (Buchbinder & Shanks, 2012; Hersh, 2010), diverse patient-centered agendas have suffered (Borkowski, 2009; National Center for Healthcare Leadership, Institute for Diversity in Health Management, American Hospital Association, & American College of Healthcare Executives, 2004).

For rural implementations associated with large and small facilities, the option to outsource their needs has remained further complicated by the inability for them to attract suitable vendors coupled with the limited finances to do so (Buchbinder & Shanks, 2012; Johnson, Murphy, McNeese, Reddy & Purao, 2013). Despite limited availability, another has been the community self-interests to secure in-house solutions (Johnson, Murphy, McNeese, Reddy & Purao, 2013). Some have proven successful through hospital-to-hospital (HHP) partnerships in which smaller rural hospitals have outsourced their HIT resource demands to larger, more technologically advanced or staffed, facilities (Johnson, Murphy, McNeese, Reddy & Purao, 2013). Lacking this alternative has resulted in decreased adoption rates (Johnson, Murphy, McNeese, Reddy & Purao, 2013). Another barrier has been the lack of IT professionals available for the maintenance, sustainability, and training of others (Hersh, 2010). This has led to exploring non-traditional model alternatives (Johnson, Murphy, McNeese, Reddy & Purao, 2013).

CTS Leadership

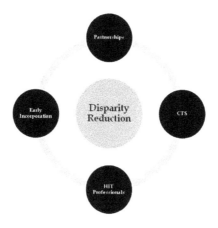

Figure 10.2

As change leaders (Kotter, 2007), in-house promotions for HIT adoption have begun within organizational cultures (Payne, Pressler, Sarkar, & Lussier, 2011). The need for drawing parallels between defined organizational HIT expectations and leadership capacities (Buchbinder & Shanks, 2012), systemic impacts, or personal optimization has remained vital (Kotter, 2007; Payne, Pressler, Sarkar, & Lussier, 2011). Through studies aimed at identifying knowledge gaps, critical factors towards informatics expertise and the supported CTS domain resources were indentified (Payne, Pressler, Sarkar, & Lussier, 2011). As represented by Figure 10.2, successful models have shown the need for these requirements to translate into organizational processes (Kotter, 2007).

Supported through informatics, evolutions into CTS have been rooted in pre-requisites of computer science (CS), biomedicine, IT, and transitional research. Despite its inclusion, or exclusion, as a form of applied mathematics versus engineering, the debate to define CS through those parameters has stood as evidence for its pre-requisite parental origins (Payne, Pressler, Sarkar, & Lussier, 2011).

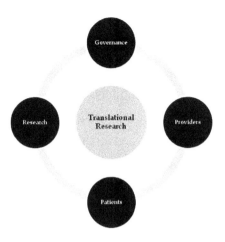

Figure 10.3

Depicted above (Figure 10.3), transitional research was spawned from researchers' abilities to take discoveries and apply them collectively towards evidence-base clinical practices through critical thinking (Payne, Pressler, Sarkar, & Lussier, 2011). Academically, the gains have remained cultural. They have included efficiency towards shared-knowledge generation through team collaboration, project planning, and data management as learning practices (Payne, Pressler, Sarkar, & Lussier, 2011).

Informatics workforce development has remained critical to integrated environments and have hinged on the ability to recruit, train, and sustain an evidence-based cycle (Payne, Pressler, Sarkar, & Lussier, 2011). Common to healthcare management in general (Buchbinder & Shanks, 2012), the success of these models has proven to be impacted by the coordination of activities and the appropriation of funding (Payne, Pressler, Sarkar, & Lussier, 2011). Regardless of organizational realm, the establishment of an academic *home* for health informatics has remained fundamental to the success of all related models (Payne, Pressler, Sarkar, & Lussier, 2011). Success has also shown to depend on the ability for organizational leadership to define and promote the required expectancies for setting educational agendas (Buchbinder & Shanks, 2012; Payne, Pressler, Sarkar, & Lussier, 2011).

Analysis

Analyzing existing members for matching comprehensive educational needs with the sought objectives defined through HITECH has proven vital (Hersh & Wright, 2010). Projected estimations for the workforce needed for the wide-spread implementation and adoption of HIT defined through HITECH were reported to be in excess of 100,000 in 2008, with future projections placed at over 200,000 by the year 2018 (Hersh, 2010; Hersh & Wright, 2010). Respecting African Americans as contributing benefactors (Hersh, 2010), the challenge has remained for them to be inclusive (Kreuter et al., 2011). However, the demand for them as contributors specific to their underserved communities has been heightened. This has resulted from the expectations for disparity reduction through HITECH initiatives coupled with the lack of an African American workforce pool from which to draw upon (Hersh & Wright, 2010; James et al, 2012).

Providers

"The Jazz science term is relevant to a lot of us because we're not just dealing with a ten year period of, of music; we're dealing with several decades."

—Courtney Pine

As the front-line enforcers (McClellan, Casalino, Shortell, & Rittenhouse, 2013), organizational and educational cultural shifts need to occur within African American provider pools (Buchbinder & Shanks, 2012). The diversity of medical specialty make-up coupled with individualized patient-centered agendas has proven impactful (Borkowski, 2009; McClellan, Casalino, Shortell, & Rittenhouse, 2013). Studies have projected the need demands for IT professional per non-IT professional to be at 1 to 56 respectively (Hersh & Wright, 2010). Interdepartmental communication, i.e. EBP and CDS, have proven to be additional motivators for patient-centered investments (McClellan, Casalino, Shortell, & Rittenhouse, 2013). Another factor has been quality insurance (QI) promotion through organizational culture (McClellan, Casalino, Shortell, & Rittenhouse, 2013).

Externally, it has been argued that the increased adoption may be aided through specialized regional assistance centers (McClellan, Casalino, Shortell, & Rittenhouse, 2013). Furthermore, it has been demonstrated that meaningful usage could be bolstered by vendors who could create HIT systems with specificity (McClellan, Casalino, Shortell, &

Rittenhouse, 2013). Studies have shown the largest needs respecting pre-requisites to be in general informatics development, management, reimbursement, and regulatory issues (Hersh & Wright, 2010; Buchbinder & Shanks, 2012). Internal and external alternative health career paths with effective provider-mentoring have been identified as factors (Borkowski, 2009; Hersh & Wright, 2010), coupled with modeling for shifting cultural consciousness to the next generation of providers (Ofili et al., 2013).

Self Assessments

Profiles based on desired technological competencies have proven useful for matching skill-sets with potentials (Borkowski, 2010; Kotter, 2007). Attempts to define pre-requisites have found that successful models incorporated evidence-based medicine (EBM) cultures into delivery schemes (Bloomrosen & Detmer, 2010; Detmer, Munger, & Lehmann, 2010). Further, it was demonstrated that modified approaches must become systemic (Hersh, 2010; Richardson et al., 2011). To satisfy the demands inherent to basic, translational, and clinical research, it has been shown that approaches respecting patient data collection coupled with its provider availability and usage must become embedded within deliveries (Bloomrosen & Detmer, 2010). The development of formal certifications to reflect competencies associated with these technical pre-requisites have become useful evaluation tools (Detmer, Munger, & Lehmann, 2010).

Organizational Culture

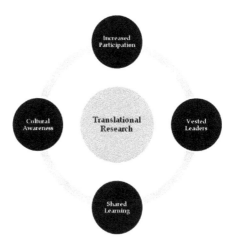

Figure 10.4

Concurrent with national costs, the community minority burdens have remained (Ofili et al., 2013). Proposals have called for an increased cultural competency coupled with strategies considering genetics and social-behavioral factors (Borkowski, 2009; Ofili et al., 2013). Respecting researchers, providers, and patients, they have also called for the promotion of a culture for shared responsibility (Bloomrosen and Detmer, 2009). As shown by Figure 10.4, cyclic feedback methods for policy guideline development of patient-centered deliveries have been advised (Bloomrosen & Detmer, 2010). The desire for fostering formal collaborations between academic research and minority serving institutions (MSI) with unique transitional research approaches have been supported (Ofili et al., 2013).

**Potential Career
Alternatives:**

BioHealth
Informaticist

BioMedical
Informaticist

Clinical Research
Informaticist

Informatics
Research Scientist

Translational
Informaticist

Chapter Eleven ▲▼▲
Cultures of Inclusion

Awareness

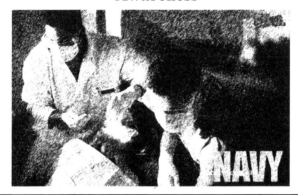

"It's not a sin to get knocked down; it's a sin to stay down"
Carl Brashear

Overview

That's me on a Navy Mobile Dental Unit (MDU) in an old promo-advertisement.   One of my most memorable re-enforcements to the importance of institutional diversity for patient-centered care occurred just prior to my entrance into the Navy as a dental officer. On that particular morning, there was to be an "all hands on deck" event. However, I was promptly informed by my department head, an African

American captain, that I would not be attending the event and was to provide clinical coverage. As a government-contracted provider at the time, this did not come surprisingly as I assumed that whatever was to be was meant for military personnel. What did come as a pleasant surprise was the patient that he escorted to me for treatment, a short time later. It was Carl Brashear, fresh from the promotion of the film *Men of Honor* (Internet Movie Database [IMDB], n.d.), which depicted his challenges to becoming the first African American Navy Master Diver (Carlbrasher.org, 2014; IMDB, 2014).

Carl Brasher withstood racial barriers and had given a limb for his contributions towards serviceable achievement. Having the opportunity to meet someone who had made such a personal sacrifice for others was fulfilling in itself. However, the deeper personal gratuity was rooted in the captain having asked me to do it. Like many civilians at that time, most of my familiarity and appreciation for Mr. Brashear's accomplishments had come from the film. But, in Navy culture he was a living legend and an *institutional* icon. He was important to *them,* regardless of my level of appreciation. Further, the mutual respect that was generated through the rare episode of diversity in that setting was reflected in the outcomes, i.e. provider-to-patient-to-administrator.

As we toiled away on his treatment, I asked him about a-lotta-stuff as anyone personally close to me throughout my years can attest to it being my way. He handled it graciously.

And, in the mist of it all, the conversation centered on the level of accuracy that was depicted in scenes of the film. He noted a few. But, more importantly, he explained that the level of meaningful intent through the presentation of a story has often proven more influential that the way it was told, i.e. its communication to the targeted audience. Mr. Brashear left with a new smile, and this encounter contributed significantly to me being militarily commissioned a short time later as a vested-stakeholder to that environment. This occurrence was a holistic example for the potential yield of cultural diversity towards patient-centered care. The following pages draw focuses the importance of integrating African American cultural perspectives into organizational processes for goal achievement.

ACHE

Adam's ARTHouse©

Respecting health care, the preamble to the American College of Healthcare Executives (ACHE) Code of Ethics, has defined ethical and legal parameters concerning the standard

135

of conduct for discrimination; hiring practices; professional and public trust; misleading communications; and abuse of power (American College of Healthcare Executives [ACHE]; Pozgar, 2013). Section I of the Code has included integrity, fairness, good faith, and complying with laws or regulations governed by the jurisdictions of multi-hospital systems (ACHE, 2011). If the lack of diversity among the make-up of medical directors has proved to be a concern for a board or governing body, the ACHE has provided ethical guidelines for diversity through several initiatives, i.e. leaders of health care management and policy statements (ACHE, 2013). These references coupled with ACHE resources offered through its toolkit have proved beneficial in avoiding organizational conflicts of ethics (ACHE, 2013). The ACHE serves as an example of a health care initiative targeted at securing equitable health delivery systems.

Emotional Intelligence

"The main thing was the social barrier of him being British and white and us being American and black. 'Cause, the thing I've noticed is a lot of black British people are still British. The things that they say and the things that they do are very British. Like, a British guy—they have their colloquiums and they are national. Whereas, our black people, we have our colloquiums and they're very regional—even inside of the black community. There are things that I say being from New Orleans—things that a black guy from Philadelphia would say

that I wouldn't know what was going on."
— Brandford Marsalis

Whether pertaining to education, research, or professional environments, the vested interests garnered from mutual respect has proven to be born from the proper alignment of vision, mission, and value oriented initiatives with those of effected stakeholders (Fryer & Greenstone, 2007; Studer, 2008). Cultures reflecting the common interests of those charged with the responsibility of carrying out processes, i.e. emotional intelligence and cultural competency, have resulted in sustainability, leadership fortitude, and trustful relationship bonds housed internally and externally (Freshman & Rubino, 2002; Fryer & Greenstone, 2007).

All have been heightened through the patient-centered initiatives defined through HITECH (HHS, 2009). To exemplify from a professional perspective, as a socially *conscience* and *conscious* health care provider, the nature of initiatives rooted in identifying educational, psychological, and moralistic deficiencies towards evidence-based treatment methods has remained motivational sources (Fox, 2006). Just as others have be able to do, initiatives common to my moralistic, spiritual, and community interests have allowed me to weather the storms of staying true to my fundamental purposes (Borkowski, 2009; Fryer & Greenstone, 2007).

Spirituality

Treatment Compliance

I have witnessed the good and adverse influential effects that religion, or spirituality, can have on a patient's health. To exemplify, a former Jehovah's Witness patient of mine once refused consent for blood work-ups prior to an extensive oral surgery appointment. The patient was a high-risk patient with several severe medical contraindications; in an infectious state, and being controlled through antibiotic therapy until definitive treatment could be rendered. To complicate matters, this patient was a ward of the state to which my department was held liable for his care, were it to be proved that the standard-of-care was breached (Pozgar, 2013). The patient eventually consented to treatment after spiritual consultation lead to an acceptable differentiation between the work-ups and a blood transfusion. These types of occurrences are common throughout the world of health care and highlight the importance for diversity respecting patient-provider perspectives for optimum treatment and mitigating risks (Borkwoski, 2009; National Center for Healthcare Leadership, Institute for Diversity in Health Management, American Hospital Association & College of Healthcare Executives, 2004).

EOL

End-of-life (EOL) care decisions of African Americans have proven to be predominantly influenced by religious and spiritual cultural influences (Mack, Paulk, Viswanath, & Prigerson, 2010). These influences have been combined with an underlying distrust of systemic health care deliveries based upon historical racism and class inequities (Thomas, Wilson, Justice, Birch, & Sheps, 2008). The cultural values of African-Americans with respect to EOL decision making has needed to be appreciated by health care administrators and professionals for reduced levels of disparity, conflict resolution, and improved choice making. The objective has been to align EOL patient preferences with the actual EOL practice trends displayed within African American communities (National Center for Healthcare Leadership, Institute for Diversity in Health Management, American Hospital Association & College of Healthcare Executives, 2004; Zheng, Mukamel, Caprio, Cai, & Temkin-Greener, 2010).

Through the Patient's Bill of Rights, ethics consultations, and committees, the patient's right to making informed decisions respecting EOL treatment options has been long established and protected through governing bodies (Pozgar, 2013). A logical assumption to the cause of differences that exist between African Americans and White Americans with respect to EOL decisions has been attributed to communication deficiencies (Kagawa-Singer, & Blackhall, 2001). To some degree, patient feedback has supported the view that communication coupled with education have proven to be factors for cultural trends of decision making (Kagawa-Singer, & Blackhall, 2001). Lack of knowledge, or misinformation, respecting advanced directives has proven influential as well, and has been reflected by their lack of usage priority within African American communities (Thomas, Wilson, Justice, Birch, & Sheps, 2008).

However, studies have shown that many African Americans rely heavily on spiritual leaders for guidance and the promise of divine intervention towards treatment outcomes (Thomas, Wilson, Justice, Birch, & Sheps, 2008). Redemption through suffering is practiced by African American Christians and viewed as a testament of faith during near death occurrences (Kagawa-Singer, & Blackhall, 2001). Their spiritual belief in God, as being the only credible source for forecasting ultimate treatment outcomes, coupled with their historical distrust of the health care system has been a primary reason for many African Americans to opt for extended care with aggressive diseased-focused treatment (Zheng, Mukamel, Caprio, Cai, & Temkin-Greener, 2010). This has been supported by the continued trend for these EOL options among African American patients (Thomas, Wilson, Justice, Birch, & Sheps, 2008), despite studies which showed evidence of effective communication prior to decision making (Mack, Paulk, Viswanath, & Prigerson, 2010).

These presentations have remained common throughout various organizational delivery systems. Therefore, a blanket policy of common moral enforcement, even among ethically identifiable like-minded provider groups, has not proven achievable regardless of general moralistic position. The overall objective for securing the major ethical principals has remained through proactive open-disclosures of practices, regardless of the environment (National Center for Healthcare Leadership, Institute for Diversity in Health Management, American Hospital Association & College of Healthcare Executives, 2004; Pozgar, 2009). Through enforced legislation of governing bodies and licensing boards, the need for moral disclosure conflicts to precede provider-patient relationships and the associated assumed duty-to-care has remained.

Through easily accessible national provider registries, moralistic treatment alternatives have been promoted. The call for providers' rights to be protected while upholding their ethical responsibilities to patient-first medical practices has also been made regardless of individual stances (Borkowski, 2009; Grady, 2006). There has remained a focus to achieve this through universally improved processes aligned with provider-patient relationships and treatment resources (National Center for Healthcare Leadership, Institute for Diversity in Health Management, American Hospital Association & College of Healthcare Executives, 2004; Pozgar, 2009). However, these examples have served to display the value that emotional intelligence respecting cultural realms has proven towards recipient trust and positive health outcomes from the patient's perspective (Das, Schwartz, & DeRenzo, 2006; National Center for Healthcare

Leadership, Institute for Diversity in Health Management, American Hospital Association & College of Healthcare Executives, 2004).

Laws and Ethics

Laws and ethics have remained integral to any initiative to be governed for respective populations. To exemplify the need for African Americans to remain inclusive respecting their implications, focus has been drawn to the confidentiality associated with the human immunodeficiency virus (HIV) and/or acquired immunodeficiency syndrome (AIDS) as they have remained health threats to our communities.

Ethics represent situational practices that are defined by the common moral culture, i.e. religious, professional, organizational, and etc., to which that individual belongs. Laws are pre-defined rules which have been established to govern the practices of individuals in society's best interest, regardless of moralistic intent. Laws and ethics often overlap. Neither is bound solely by the other (Pozgar, 2013; Rowe & Moodley, 2013). Many ethical challenges exist for providers, i.e. physicians, nurses, and health care administrators, attempting to secure patient privacy and treatment while preserving organizational safety (Pozgar, 2013). Without a cure for HIV/AIDS, providers who have reduced the emotional strain and stigma normally attached to it while maintaining hope through comfort-based treatment options, have displayed beneficence. Justice has been displayed by those who have assisted in access-to-care or administered standard-of-care treatment deliveries that were not precluded by moral judgments. Autonomy has proven relevant in the personal patient choices of desired treatment options versus the refusal of treatment for diseased states (Pozgar, 2013; Rowe & Moodley, 2013).

Tort law has proven to be the primary kind of law associated with HIV/AIDS cases. Unintentional torts, i.e. negligence, have been associated with diagnostics, regimens of medicine, and test results (Pozgar, 2013). Negligence of providers and organizations, by failing to practice proven methods for decreasing risks and the spread of disease, has also been associated with the disease (Pozgar, 2013; Rowe & Moodley, 2013). Intentional torts, i.e. patient isolations and character defamation, are also potential liabilities (Pozgar, 2013). Ethics and laws have often proven to be at odds with each other. A common ground of sound ethical practices, supported by legal principles with moral enforcements, is needed to insure the quality and safety of comprehensive health care (Pozgar, 2013; Rowe & Moodley, 2013).

Cultures of Inclusion

Chapter Twelve ▲
AFRO Education

Home Schoolin'

"You're better than I was at your age.
If I haven't accomplished that, then I
haven't been doing my job"

● My father when I was a boy

Overview

My father, now retired, was educated as a mathematician. In addition to toiling away with me during math and science homework assignments or tech-hobbies throughout my youth, he was employed within a computer systems center as a federal employee for a government agency throughout the 60's, 70's, and 80's. Like most boys, he was my in-house hero, so you can see the significance of those words being expressed to me. And unknowingly to him, he was culturally instilling in me the true meaning of fatherhood, mentorship, and the purpose for cultural-evolution. Specifically, that is the love, courage and capacity to acknowledge one's limitations, regardless of past accomplishments for the betterment of future generations. Further, this is a social application of EBP. In that respect, everyday, I've tried to be like my father. The following pages draw significance to cultural impacts on African American educational community development.

Racial Identity and Centrality

"When your history becomes longer than your future
you gain a new perspective of the significance of living
through the plethora of things that helped to shape
and define your being."
— Jae Sinnett

The theoretical equivalents to emotional intelligence and cultural competency that have been deemed applicable throughout the spectrum of higher learning are racial identity and centrality. Racial identity has represented the qualitative significance that one has attributed to their membership within the Black racial group within their self-concepts (Sellers, Smith, Shelton, Rowley, & Chavous, 1998). Applications have been defined through a multidimensional model of racial identity (MMRI) based on 4 dimensions to include centrality, regard, salience, and the related identity to a person's race. (Hurd et al., 2012; Sellers, Smith, Shelton, Rowley, & Chavous, 1998).

Racial centrality has come to represent the level to which individuals define themselves respecting their race, i.e. positive or negative perceptions, and membership (Fryer & Greenstone, 2007; Hurd et al., 2012). Being a socially constructed concept, the arbitrary categorization of race has resulted in the psychological unification of individuals with varied experiences and cultural expressions (Sellers, Smith, Shelton, Rowley, & Chavous, 1998). Similar to the underlying purposes for patient-centered medicine (Varkey, 2010), these approaches have served collectively to build understanding towards the development of vested stakeholders for educational agendas, curriculums, and achievement (Fryer & Greenstone, 2007; Hernandez et al., 2013; Hurd et al., 2012; Kruter et al., 2011; Ofili et al., 2013).

Mindsets

"Get up boy and pee on a rock. It ain't quite day but, it's 4 O'clock!" — my uncle

I've awakened to that quote on every visit with my uncle, a WWII veteran and former school teacher, since I was about 5 or 6 years old. It was how we started the day. He worked in tandem with my dad as my second father. And like my dad, traditional contact with him throughout my life has remained daily or weekly more times than not. As a humorous aside, I distinctly remember riding to my maternal grandfather's farm house in Culpeper, VA. He and I walked into Daddy Yager's living room and I was promptly asked, "You gotta job yet?" —I was about 5 years old. 8 acres on a tractor in the sun and a straw hat, is cool on your granddaddy's lap when you're small. But trust me; the training session can be short-lived. These types of occurrences, and there many of them, framed my mindset. And, for me, that's what it's all about.

Studies have proven African American achievement to be attributable to individual mindsets. It has been shown that individuals who have held the belief that their abilities are adaptable have greater goal-oriented success rates (Hernandez et al., 2013). This factor has remained significant due to the influence that internal or external institutional factors have proven towards framing the individual mindsets of African Americans (Fryer & Greenstone, 2007; Hernandez et al., 2013; Hurd et al., 2012; Kruter et al., 2011; Ofili et al., 2013). My uncle, and fraternity brother, also told me that he sunk a whale with his military medals while standing on a ship. But, that's a story for another day.

Community Culture

"Later on, as I got into high school. Initially, I didn't know that that was going to be an option for me. In my younger years, I don't know if I really thought so much about college, but when I got into high school, it seemed that I had the aptitude for at least the academics."
— James Watkins

As one of the first African American dentists to graduate from the Medical College of Virginia and past president of the Virginia Dental Board of Health Professions, Dr. Watkins further explained the impacts of community towards cultural development:

A real sense of community? Of course! I guess the one thing, that you even hear about now, is we didn't have just one parent. We had a bunch of parents living in the projects. You couldn't do anything without someone knowing what you were doing and that you are James Watkins' son, at such and such a place, especially if you weren't supposed to be there (Virginia Tech, 2000).

Like-wise, from the cultural perspective of African Americans as beneficiaries to health and education initiatives, the social contexts governing computer utilization and HIT acceptance have remained a concern (McNeill, Puleo, Bennett, & Emmons, 2007; Montague & Perchonok, 2012). Though the disparity gap respecting computer ownership for African Americans is narrowing, health disparities have been proven to be linked to lack of information, i.e. educational and health, to affected populations coupled with their ability to interpret and apply that information usefully (McNeill et al., 2007; Montague & Perchonok, 2012). A lack of attention to this has proven a formidable barrier to optimizing the tools afforded through HIT towards preventions, chronic diseases, and management (HHS, 2013; Montague & Perchonok, 2012).

Wellness Informatics

Computers have served as an indispensable educational tool for shared medical knowledge (HHS, 2013). A focus has been drawn to disseminating culturally centered health information to underserved populations, as it has been demonstrated that information adapted in that fashion has led to modified behavior towards cultures of prevention (Montague & Perchonok, 2012). A Health Information

National Trends Survey (HINTS) has shown that more than 60% of African Americans used online resources for access to health information (HHS, 2013; McNeill et al., 2007). It has also been demonstrated that the desire for usage among African American youth and older adults is similar. For initiatives to be advantageous, the desire to incorporate the need for learning the skills to do so into community cultures has remained (HHS, 2013; McNeill et al., 2007). Wellness informatics has served as an example through technological applications used primarily by the consumer and independent of the health care system, i.e. computers and other media (Montague & Perchonok, 2012).

PHR
Culture

As previously explained in prior chapters, being similar to the EHR for post-care electronic documentation, the universally available personal health record (PHR) has allowed patients to catalogue individual treatments from *their* perspective. In turn, this information has assisted patients in their ability to relay past histories to providers for collaboration with EHRs and comprehensive diagnosis and treatment options (Hebda & Czar, 2013; Montague & Perchonok, 2012).

Chapter Thirteen ▲
AFRO Self

Adam's ARTHouse©

"I had a strong foundation growing up; my parents were loving, affectionate people. Ever since I can remember, my father was always hugging and kissing us.
He would say *give me those jaws*"
(his term for kissing our cheeks)
● Muhammad Ali

Overview

As the previous chapters have shown, many initiatives respecting diversity and inclusion have been established. However, just as with past educational, professional, and community-oriented strategies, the need for African Americans to remain inclusive to insure that those securities are not breeched, i.e. non-intentionally or intentionally, has remained. Further, this necessity has been reflected throughout the entire professional spectrum; as African American representation has remained lacking at entry level positions for executive leadership careers (Schwartz & Cooper, 2013; Journal of Blacks in Higher Education [JBHE], 2014).

Pauline Higgins, an African American lawyer, former partner and chief diversity officer at Thomas & Knight, stated in the NY Times, "You don't want to be a diversity officer who only buys tables at events and seats people. It's about recruiting and inclusion and training and development, with substantive work assignments." Higgins also explained that since her leaving the committee in 2008, the subsequent lack of representation has resulted in fewer meetings and fewer African American lawyers at the firm (Schwartz & Cooper, 2013). Dr. Irving P. McPhail (2012), CEO of the National Action Council for Minorities in Engineering, has supported these sentiments:

Now more than ever, the nation's changing demographics demand that we include all of our citizens in science and engineering education and careers. For the U.S. to benefit from the diverse talents of all its citizens, we must grow the pipeline of qualified, underrepresented minority engineers and scientists to fill positions in industry and academia (National Academy of Engineering, 2014; Valla & Williams, 2012).

The sincere call for responsible solutions has remained inherent to our community. Representatives of opposing views concerning resolutions to common barriers for progress have continued to be expressed. Through socially-based reasoning, esteemed philosopher Cornell West has advocated for more equitable distribution for years. In *Race Matters* (1993), Dr. West argued, "We have created rootless, dangling people with little link to the supportive networks—family, friends, and school—that sustain some sense of purpose in life." As the former president of the National Bar Association, John Page (Schwartz & Cooper, 2013), explained that "There is diversity fatigue. We could fall backwards very quickly." The Wall Street Journal editorial board member Jason L. Riley, through Ogbu's research (Ogbu, 2003), explained that the racial gap respecting education, to include math, reading, SAT and other standardized tests scores, for African Americans versus other groups has widened and proved a significant impact to our overall lack of progress. Further, he pointed out that Ogbu's studies found the issue spread among economic class statuses, to include those of black professionals. Collectively, both made the argument(s) that despite the opportunities afforded through legislation; institutional black culture, i.e. community, educational, and organizational, has remained the predominant contributor. Riley also used similar reasoning respecting the work-force to support his arguments against affirmative action (Riley, 2014).

Love, through familiarity, has often bred contempt out of concern, ambition, frustration, and commitment. And the self-love for our people expressed through opposing views should not be dismissed among us. That being said, for me, the theoretical answers have continued to lay somewhere in between. As a product of the era, I have continued to believe that the gains afforded through civil rights legislation, to include affirmative action, where and, to some degree, still remain necessary components of our comprehensive treatment plan for racially-based injustice and disparity. However, I have also held true to the theory that neither social responsibility nor personal self-worth has proven to be effectively legislated towards the establishment of *truly*-vested stakeholders, regardless of the infrastructure for opportunity that has been *sacrificed* or established to do so. Though a significant threat from disparity has remained to be addressed, I pose that enough bricks have been secured for our communities to build towards responsible empowerment through education by exhausting available resources; while re-affirming our rights to use them through commitment, established laws, governance and advocacy. *Achievement* has remained *fundamental* to *responsible outreach.*

Advocacy

US health care system policies are decision-based platforms that change patient experiences. Ideas, originating from its constituents (IOM, 1999), are presented at the state or national level (IOM, 2001), developed and enacted in the legislative branch, and implemented through the executive branches of government respectively (HHS, 2009). Because reform advocacy is often politically driven, complexities of broad-based strategies have been traditionally hampered by bipartisanship, disease-focused isolations, and the inherent fragmentations of these ideologies (Borkowski, 2009; Panel on Measuring Medical Care Risk in Conjunction with the New Supplemental Income Poverty Measure, 2007; Richardson et al., 2011). Despite these limitations, health care professionals can be influential in reform enactment through various resources; drawn from their own experiences, and in partnership with fellow constituents and organizations of like-minded agendas. While calling for reform, the American Cancer Society has served as an example by setting a precedent for identifying an isolated disease occurrence as the primary and direct result of a national health care systemic-deficiency (American Cancer Society, 2014). In this spirit, focus will be drawn to opportunities for policy reform and advocacy by health care professionals.

Reform

As educational and strategic consultants, providers and administrators are invaluable assets to policy makers, many of whom are unfamiliar with inner-workings of health care systems and outcomes (IOM, 1999; IOM, 2001). As active participants expressing their advocacy through various realms, i.e. board membership and advisory staff, health care professionals can influence the policy development within various levels of health care reform implementation (Barton, 2010; HHS, 2009).

Professional Education
and
Licensure

Regardless of focus, effective reform has often incorporated the promotion of cultural-shifts aimed at reducing targeted deficiencies to their root causes (McFadden, Stock, & Gowen, 2011). Active and direct participation in the development of up-and-coming professional students as faculty, or through mentorship, have demonstrated their effectiveness to influence practice-purpose and competency levels with respect to technology, informatics, identification of disparities, and quality assurance (Barton, 2010). Acknowledging that policy development within state and national licensure boards has often dictated health professional curriculums, both educational and licensure venues have proven effective as reform influences (VDHP, 2013).

Community Campaigns

Successful campaigns and strategies for rural or community health settings have served as examples of how issues may be fenced and adapted to specific communities or population needs (Schaetti et al., 2012). These strategies have the potential to serve as modifiable evidence-based templates for nation-wide reform agendas (IOM, 2001; Schaetti et al., 2012).

National and State

Health professionals have proven a responsibility for adhering to national reform platforms in the better interest of society's whole (Barton, 2010; HHS, 2009). While proposing evidence-based solutions, inherent to these responsibilities are the professional obligations to identifying reform deficiencies while working with government agencies, in the spirit of non-partisan good intent, to support successful implementations of effectiveness (Nunez-Smith et al., 2011).

AFRO Self

Chapter Fourteen ▲

AFRO Change

"Young, ardent and hopeful, I entered upon this new life in the full gush of unsuspecting enthusiasm. The cause was good, the men engaged in it were good, the means to attain its triumph, good."

● Frederick Douglass

Overview

After his freedom, Frederick Douglass was speaking on personal initiatives for change towards becoming an agent of advocacy for a society of abolitionists (Douglass, 2013). Traditionally, organizational changes in education, research, or health care have been defined through attempts by administrators to control rising cost while integrating policy, oversight legislation, and remaining true to their respective initiatives (Borkowski, 2009; Joshi & Perin, 2012; Kreuter et al., 2011). Successful organizational environments have remained dynamic and driven through various external and internal impacts (Buchbinder & Shanks, 2012; James, Starks, Segrest, & Burke, 2012; Kotter, 2007).

Drivers

Social and industrial environments represent external drivers that have often signaled a need for organizational adaptation, i.e. collaboration or partnerships (Franklin et al., 2012). To remain viable, these approaches have been used to address economic trends, service expansion, or to satisfy government requirements (Borkowski, 2009; Franklin et al., 2012). Respecting resources for education, research, and social development, collaborations of stakeholders of common interests have proved productive (James, Starks, Segrest, & Burke, 2012; Ofili et al., 2014). Internal drivers for change have been defined through personnel shortages, resources, financial deficiencies, community, educational, and health delivery improvements (Borkowski, 2009; Franklin et al., 2012; Ofili et al., 2014).

Readiness

Change readiness has remained a multi-leveled and multi-faceted dynamic (Weiner, 2009). Grass-roots innovations and evidence-based changes have proven vital to policy-based initiatives. These have been rooted in efficiency, quality, and sustainability through individuals, groups, units, departments, and organizational strategies (Martin, Weaver, Currie, Finn, & McDonald, 2012; Ofili et al., 2014; Weiner, 2009). These elements have proven to be fundamental to sustained cultural shifts (Borkowski, 2009). Change successes have been supported through the shared psychological states of stakeholders (Hernandez et al., 2013; Weiner, 2009), with satisfaction and morale vital to successful implementations (Borkowski, 2009; Franklin et al., 2012; Fryer & Greenstone, 2007).

Reduced ambiguities coupled with explanations of change values remain driving forces behind successful initiatives (Hurd, Sánchez, Zimmerman, & Caldwell, 2013; Martin et al., 2012). Effective change implementations by educational, research, and professional organizational members have been associated with the common factors of high readiness levels that have led to greater effort, persistence, and cooperation (James, Starks, Segrest, & Burke, 2012; Weiner, 2009).

Leadership

P.Y. Wyatt
1959

"This suggests a path to peace and mutual respect
which both White and Colored Virginians can
pursue with benefits to the Commonwealth"
— Roy Wilkins

That quote came in a letter to my grandfather in 1959, which I read some time later after his death in an old article clipping during my college days. Its purpose remains significant to me because my grandfather, from Charlottesville, VA, had to leave home at a very early age to further his education. As a child, and with it having little meaning to me at the time, I was made aware of that circumstance on a visit with him back to his old homestead. The house was just a block or two from the University of Virginia. The relative importance of that fact grew throughout my teenage years; and culminated with me reading that quote as I came to realize that after over 30 years of serving as a minority dentist, mentor, and civil activist at local and state levels, Dr. Wyatt was able to celebrate the official integration of schools in his former community as the state president of the NAACP. His vested interest, instilled from youth, had come full circle. Further, his leadership style was quiet spoken, yet firm. His demeanor towards problem focused approaches afforded him the mutual respect needed from stakeholders during partnerships for other state-wide community advancements, i.e. university de-segregations and bi-racial committees (Coder Fitzgerald, 1979; George Mason University, 1971). More importantly, for me, he stood as the ultimate role-model for responsible outreach through achievable leadership. And to us, he was just *Granddaddy*.

Leadership presents in various styles and manners. The promotion of competencies and standards aimed at quality improvement, leadership, and safety for better health outcomes (Barton, 2010), has been demonstrated through such entities as the National Center for Healthcare Leadership (NCHL, 2014), or through the ACHE's aforementioned *Code of Ethics* (ACHE, 2011). However, the need and continued willingness for potential leadership to seek and utilize tools for undergoing sincere evaluations of their leadership styles, i.e. strengths, weaknesses, cultural competency, and racial identity for increased effectiveness, has remained (Borkowski, 2009; Fryer & Greenstone, 2007).

Characteristics

Strengths

Specific parameters defined through a competency or standard have proven useless without executives, administrators, providers, and professionals empowered and/or willing to execute effectively within those guidelines (ACHE, 2011), or demonstrating the leadership required to do so (Kotter, 2011). The ability to align and combine the various approaches to leadership, i.e. styles and methods, with the ever-changing dynamics inherent to traditional health care environments has proven useful to successful implementations of change (Borkowski, 2009; Buchbinder & Shanks, 2012).

Limitations

As mentioned earlier, increases in cultural competency and diversity have been clearly defined as objectives targeted by health care organizations (Borkowski, 2009). Various organizations have employed tools for self-assessments towards these ends (Fryer & Greenstone, 2007; National Center for Healthcare Leadership, Institute for Diversity in Health Management, American Hospital Association, & College of Healthcare Executives, 2004). The aim for effective minority leadership has proven to be a cyclic reassessment of one's leadership effectiveness respecting goal initiatives (National Center for Healthcare Leadership, Institute for Diversity in Health Management, American

Hospital Association, & College of Healthcare Executives, 2004; Studer, 2008).

Figure 14.1

Community Level

Reliable access to quality care has remained a common barrier to urban and rural delivery systems (Barton, 2010; Johnson, Murphy, McNeese, Reddy, & Purao, 2013). As illustrated above (Figure 14.1), successful pro-active interventions have often begun in lower educational models (Hurd, Sánchez, Zimmerman, & Caldwell, 2013), and been rooted in identifiable cultural, sociological, and health status needs (James, Starks, Segrest, & Burke, 2012). To exemplify respecting African American communities, historically black colleges and universities (HBCUs) have built a cultural allegiance to support their attendance based on purposes rooted in the needs of their stakeholders, i.e. learning approaches, social inclusion and acclimation. Despite a long-standing struggle for economic sustainability, an established culture of meaningful purpose has existed (Fryer & Greenstone, 2007).

Educational Level

"I believe the children are our future. Teach them well and
let them lead the way"
— George Benson

The sustainability of culturally-established models has remained tied to social infrastructure improvements (Joshi, Puricelli Perin, 2012). In African American communities, cultural patterns coupled with methods for educational and career development have proven vital (Fryer & Greenstone, 2007; James, Starks, Segrest, & Burke, 2012). I discussed the matter with a life-long friend and professional colleague. Steven Miller, M.A., a mental health administrator for over 20 years and currently a Care Manager/Critical Time Intervention Coordinator for the DC Department of Behavioral Health (S. B. Miller, personal communication), commented concerning the positive framing for greater academic and professional achievement respecting our youth:

There is an African Proverb which states, *until the lion has a historian, the hunter will be the hero.* Simply put, my posterity, never rely on your oppressors to define who or what you are, and tell your story! For if you do; you will always be the conquered, and not the conqueror.

Further, the evidence has supported this. It has been shown that beginning in adolescents; approaches to academic performance need to be structured to reflect realistic and purposeful career paths (Fryer & Greenstone, 2007; Muller, Riegle-Crumb, Schiller, Wilkinson, & Frank, 2010). This was demonstrated in mathematics curriculums, early prerequisites to CTS (Payne, Pressler, Sarkar, & Lussier, 2011), in which reduced stratification with increased exposure produced significant long-term academic increases in performance (Muller, Riegle-Crumb, Schiller, Wilkinson, & Frank, 2010).

Figure 14.2

Educators

"Anybody can help make a brilliant student successful.
But I think it requires a special talent to take a student who
requires more, and make them successful."
— Harold Marioneaux.

Depicted above (Figure 14.2), researchers have called for academic leadership to remain engaged as partners for developing the appropriate curricula for desired pre-requisites (Ofili et al., 2013). Studies have concluded that educational informatics goals should be well-defined through collaborative early interventions, and based on key core-competencies (Kampov-Plevoi & Hemminger, 2011). The potential for modified educational infrastructures was demonstrated by mentored African American adolescents exposed to early intervention methods (Hurd, Sánchez, Zimmerman, & Caldwell, 2013).

As an advocate for educational development, Dr. Marioneaux, former dean at Hampton University's School of Science and now the Founding Director of Thomas Nelson Community College's Dental Hygiene Program, has served as an example by developing the AP Max System. The web based system can be used on any educational level, and improves student performance through academic evaluation while addressing targeted deficiencies. Past applications have been credited with student entries into post-graduate professional schools at a rate of 92% (Daily Press, 2005).

Mentorships

if music is the most universal language
just think of me as one whole note

— Nikki Giovanni

Professor Giovanni was speaking from her poem titled, *Communication* (Giovanni, 1997). I thought it to be apropos because the efforts of natural mentors, i.e. supportive non-parental adults, have proven to raise the level of students' personal investments. This applied to adolescents and high school youth, through the ability to communicate associations between personal perceptions, goals, barriers, and achievement (Hurd, Sánchez, Zimmerman, & Caldwell, 2013).

Studies showed that students thrived when adequate academic preparation was coupled with focused program supplementations of community vested interests (Kreuter et al., 2011).

Professional Level

The need to identify best practices realized for meaningful use by professionals has been proven (McClellan, Casalino, Shortell, & Rittenhouse, 2013). It has been shown that the key to their adoption was a desire to respond to individual and population needs (Joshi & Puricelli Perin, 2012; Kreuter et al., 2011). To exemplify, Dr. Dwight McMillan, Founding Director of Carolina Dentac in South Carolina (D. McMillan, personal communication, December 27, 2014), realized the necessity for provider-led implementation initiatives early in his career. He became proactive, and in a recent interview to me expressed:

When going into private practice back in 1997, office computing and automation was beginning to emerge as an important component of office management. I quickly realize how advantageous it would be for auxiliary staff to be technologically proficient as networking became more popular. This would leave the clinician to focus on patient care.

Commenting on steps he took to complement his personal education towards provider HIT clinical proficiency, he further explained his initiatives:

The standard dental assistant curriculum at the time did not address this major development; therefore, I developed the D.C.T. curriculum and established Carolina Dentac to promote and deliver it. As of this publication, current changes in our Healthcare System are largely centered on the implementation of technology, the same focal point I recognized 18 years earlier. Thus, it was a natural progression to offer Electronic Health Record (EHR) support for dental clinicians as an online portal through our website.

Respecting that, comprehensive strategies for communicating the direct correlations between adoption and serviceable needs for African Americans have remained to be established (Borkowski, 2009; McClellan, Casalino, Shortell, & Rittenhouse, 2013).

AFRO Change

Chapter Fifteen ▲▼▲
AFRO Plan

The upward pull through trained leadership;
the character-begetting power of strong
personalities, the inspirations to higher ideals,
to self master, to efficient service through
genuine leadership must be recognized.
Where there is no vision the people perish."

● Hallie Quinn Brown

Rationale

In her speech, *Not Gifts but Opportunity* (McFarlin, 1975, p. 176), Professor Brown further explained that "without such teachers, helpers, and leaders, the schools and colleges must fail and the race sink to lower levels. No stream can rise higher that its source". The call for expanding informatics into general education disciplines has been made by various stakeholders (Collins & Weiner, 2010; Hersh & Wright, 2010). Respecting that, my personal aim has been to target educational and health disparities by helping to insure that our African American communities remain inclusive through early cultural modifications. In doing so, a method for drawing the parallels between accepted informatics pre-requisites (Hersh, 2010; Hersh & Wright, 2010), and similar pre-requisites related to educational disparity reduction, i.e. science, technology, and health, for African Americans was developed (Hurd et al., 2013; James et al., 2012; Kreuter et al., 2011; Muller et al., 2010).

This dynamic was addressed by searching for theoretical and empirical study literature, i.e. clinical and action-based (Aveyar, 2010). The objective was to gain a broad perspective of pre-requisite exposure, recruitment, and attrition schemes throughout the entire educational spectrum (Hurd et al., 2013; James et al., 2012; Kreuter et al., 2011; McClellan et al., Muller et al., 2010). Defined searches were performed through the US National Library of Medicine (NIH/NLM, 2014). Usage was guided by peer-reviewed studies of related theoretical assumptions targeted at African American disparity reduction(s), followed by empirical studies, i.e. qualitative and quantitative methods, to investigate the validity of those assumptions. An attempt was made to identify references made to comprehensive studies, i.e. successes and failures, for eliminating assumed theoretical biases while identifying worthy contributors (Aveyar, 2010). The search study classifications and supporting rationale that guided this methodical review for analysis have been subsequently provided.

Needs

Characteristics

Successful models have shown their ability to identify, align, and communicate the established prerequisites as desirable personal goals (Hurd, Sánchez, Zimmerman, & Caldwell, 2013). This was supported by the IOM in calls for a rapid learning health care system. Through EBM, the cyclic model called for translational evidence to be made available for adapting to specific end-uses (Bloomrosen & Detmer, 2010). Its feedback mechanism has promoted the cultural integration of informatics through its availability to academic organizations, researchers, providers, policy makers, HIT professionals, and patients for patient-centered care (Bloomrosen & Detmer, 2010; Borkowski, 2009; Cliff, 2012).

Early Education

Successful models from the early alignment of stakeholder interests have spanned the entire spectrum of higher learning (Hurd, Sánchez, Zimmerman, & Caldwell, 2013). Returning to the example respecting adolescent mathematics, it was concluded that the structure of learning opportunity being offered was impactful for long-lasting achievement (Muller, Riegle-Crumb, Schiller, Wilkinson, & Frank, 2010). Studies demonstrated that the early integration to promote the inclusion of African American students increased the sustained participation in future disciplines, i.e. high school curriculum (Muller, Riegle-Crumb, Schiller, Wilkinson, & Frank, 2010). The early and accurate projection of resources has been required (Hersh & Wright, 2010).

Figure 15.1

Post-graduate

Increased care, prevention, and satisfaction have been reported by patients who received care from providers of common race and ethnicity (Kreuter et al., 2011). The referenced study respecting African American public health recruitment, explored models that framed specific matters of community interests (Figure 15.1). Through the Eliminating Health Disparities Pre-Doctoral Fellowship Program, a multifaceted approach was delivered through targeted fellowships concerning disparity reduction. Among other reported outcomes, the significances included; culturally embedding awareness resulted in a heightened sense of purpose; program participation became competitive as the related benefits became evident; effective student-centric approaches were produced by vested leaders for those with non-ideal academic exposures; and the production of shared learning exchanges (Kreuter et al., 2011).

Potentials

"Overall, I think the main thing a musician would like to do is give a picture to the listener of the many wonderful things that he knows of and senses in the universe. That's what I would like to do. I think that's one of the greatest things you can do in life and we all try to do it in some way. The musician's is through his music."

— John Coltrane

The recruitment of potential African American contributors to health related workforces aimed at disparity reduction has proven to be bolstered by meaningful purposes aligned with organizational needs (Borkwoski, 2009; Kreuter et al., 2011). Guided by established educational pre-requisites, successful models for establishing inter-institutional partnerships between organizations have been recorded (Ofili et al., 2014). One example showed the importance for embedding diversity within organizational objectives by delivering a framework for biomedical research workforce development (Borkowski, 2009; Ofili et al., 2014).

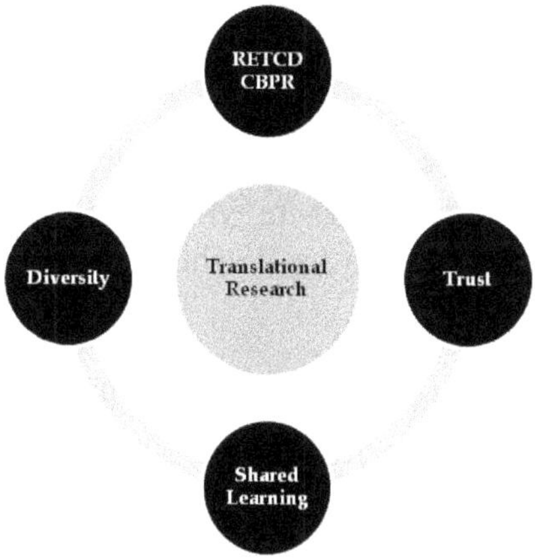

Afroinformatics™

Figure 15.2

The Collaborative Research Education, Training and Career Development (RETCD) included targeted funding resources for disparities focused work, statistical support, and investigator mentorship, while producing effective partnerships between HBCUs and Minority Serving Institutions (Ofili et al., 2014). Other models based on Community-Based Participatory Research (CBPR) methodology, have reduced the associated mistrust (James, Starks, Segrest, & Burke, 2012). As shown above (Figure 15.2), all have served as evidence-based examples that the proper alignment of organizational and personal goals could increase the potential for positive recruitment of African American stakeholders (Borkowski, 2009; James, Starks, Segrest, & Burke, 2012; Ofili et al., 2014).

HIT Competencies

"I want to be able to visit any genre and
converse there with my horn."
— Grover Washington, Jr.

For this, a review based on a query of the HIMSS Analytical Database performed in 2008 to contribute to the accurate projection of HIT was used (Hersh, 2010). Other key factors that have proven critical are the quantified and characteristically defined pre-requisites for competency (Hersh, 2010). For African-Americans, insufficient and inclusive buy-ins to technology has proven attributable to the lack of early exposure through curriculums (Hurd, Sánchez, Zimmerman, & Caldwell, 2013). Studies have demonstrated that post-secondary minority students have often fallen victim to mistrust (James, Starks, Segrest, & Burke, 2012). Additionally, Hersh & Wright (2010) argued that the data required to obtain accurate numbers for professionals existing within biomedical informatics has remained limited. Their review analyzed quantitative and qualitative data for defining informatics pre-requisites, and was chosen to highlight the potential for matching educational needs with the objectives (Hersh & Wright, 2010).

Benefits

Though comprehensively undefined, objectives have been established for desired competency levels, i.e. educational value, promotion, and innovative learning environments (Hersh & Wright, 2010). Remaining vital has been the ability to establish those as desirable ambitions towards vested professionals (Borkowski, 2009; Buchbinder & Shanks, 2012; Hurd, Sánchez, Zimmerman, & Caldwell, 2013). Spanning the entire educational spectrum, mentored adolescent students exposed to models of early intervention displayed a better acceptance for higher-level demands (Hurd, Sánchez, Zimmerman, & Caldwell, 2013). This also held in studies of math outcome performances aimed at showing the effects of stratification on underserved minority high school students (Muller, Riegle-Crumb, Schiller, Wilkinson, & Frank, 2010). Both exemplified a core critical thinking subject common to specified informatics pre-requisites, i.e. statistics. Those of post-secondary education, have proven better committed to disparity reduction schemes (Kreuter et al., 2011) or HIT initiatives if the benefits of doing so have been made personal (Borkowski, 2009; McClellan, Casalino, Shortell, & Rittenhouse, 2013).

AFRO Plan

Chapter Sixteen
AFRO Action

> "Let's trace the birth of an idea. It's born as rampant radicalism, then it becomes progressivism, then liberalism, then it becomes moderate, conservative, outmoded, and gone."
>
> ● Adam Clayton Powell, Jr.

Closing Thoughts

Like those before us, I am not the holder of any *guaranteed* solutions. For me, my community related ambitions have been a series of highs and lows that have run concurrent with life's personal challenges and proved common to many of us. Professionally, I have orchestrated hundreds of thousands in profitable returns as a solo-practitioner, received awards as a military officer for my participation in access to patient care, and also been forced to succumb in the mist of financial turmoil. In fact, this project began on the heels of my failed attempt to establish a pre-health tech-training clinic for dental services that I was forced to close in the aftermath of

185

the 2008 economic crisis. And, like many other business owners of that time, I am still licking my wounds. But, having been born in 1964, I am a product of the social, institutional, and governmental systemic influences of our nation. I attended public K-12 schools and HBCUs for my undergraduate and doctoral degrees. I have continued to further my education through online post-graduate university resources. And though not a beneficiary to extravagant life-styles, more times than not, I have been fortunate enough to achieve set goals throughout a career that has afforded me an appreciable quality of life. I consider myself the common black professional. For that, I have remained grateful.

Beginning in 1993, I have directly applied the majority of the aforementioned material in all of those settings to remain viable. 20 years ago, my initial explorations into what has become known as informatics were successful attempts to merge old digital imaging/DICOM systems with rudimentary practice management software onto Windows 3.1 operating systems. Technology has afforded me the ability to level the playing field, so-to-speak, for utilizing resources, i.e. financial, human, and equipment, which have often only been made accessible to larger community populations. This work has been rooted in my firm belief for the cultural inclusion of informatics towards the significant reduction of African American disparities throughout the entire spectrum of our interests, i.e. educational, health, and economic prosperity. Further, I am not alone in standing behind this rationale or billions of dollars in resources would not have been allocated over the last 15 or so years for providing others with the opportunity to utilize them. So, to sum it up humorously in a manner of logic common to my Hood brothers...*how 'bout we seize that opportunity for a change?*

It has been accepted that internal and external cultural changes are required for meeting the workforce requirements of large scale HIT implementations (Borkowki, 2009; Montague & Perchonok, 2012). To realize the "culture of shared responsibility", the AMIA called for educational schemes aimed at related areas including basic computer programming, health informatics, health services research, population health, and comparative effectiveness (Bloomrosen & Detmer, 2010). Through cultural competencies (Hersh & Wright, 2010; Johnson, Murphy, McNeese, Reddy, & Purao, 2013), successful adaptations have maintained a productive level of social awareness (Borkowski, 2009; Joshi & Puricelli Perin, 2012).

To include African Americans, cultural re-definitions for educational development have also shown to be needed (Fryer & Greenstone, 2007; Hersh & Wright, 2010; Kreuter et al., 2011). Learning approaches should use the educational expectations defined through these programs to be incorporated early into educational schemes for career path alternatives. Not to prominently embed these considerations within the targeted *theoretical* resolutions for disparity reduction (James, Starkes, Segrest, & Burke, 2012; Johnson, Murphy, McNeese, Reddy, & Purao, 2013), would result in the continued cyclic promotion of the dreaded sacrificial burden of choice common to many, if not the majority, of aspiring African American professional students. Specifically, the choice of having to ignore their vested community interests to remain sustainable (Fryer & Greenstone, 2007; Kreuter, 20011; James et al., 2012).

Successful models have shown the benefits from framing effective learning cultures to expected certifications and EBM (Bloomrosen & Detmer, 2010; Detmer, Munger, & Lehmann, 2010). It has been demonstrated that global informatics developments for professionals on a localized scale can be achieved through partnerships between health centers and local institutions to form learning centers for public health systems (Joshi & Puricelli Perin, 2012). It has also been shown that potential models for existing professionals could be realized through community site partnerships to establish alternative HIT career paths (James et al., 2012; McClellan, Casalino, Shortell, & Rittenhouse, 2013).

The need for higher learning initiatives to include a culturally diverse, national collaborative for leveraging the infrastructure and resources towards successful pathways was displayed (James et al., 2012; Kampov-Polevoi & Hemminger, 2011; Ofili et al., 2013). The evidence has suggested that the early incorporation of informatics into the social, educational, and professional development of African Americans is vital to successful strategies for disparity reduction (Hurd et al., 2013; James et al., 2012; Muller et al.,

2010). To that end, a national collaborative effort between academic institutions and health organizations for defined career roles and competencies, coupled with established evidence-based curriculums aimed at health, education, and economic disparity reduction for African American communities has remained warranted.

AFRO Action

Postface

My mother died from cancer, just as I was closing the final chapter on the first half-century of my life. Her skin and eyes were of a Diane Nash tone and complexion. Her hair was Malcolm-X red. A month and a half before her passing, she prepared her annual Thanksgiving meal for a blended 20 plus family mix, and in the spirit of our great "Aunt T", welcomed whoever showed up. That's who she was.

Among other endeavors, my mother was an administrator for an HBCU for roughly 20 years. However, until I began junior-high school, she was the stay-at-homemaker with the exception of substitute teaching at the neighborhood elementary school. During this time, it was her that told me *you can do it... there is nothing better than a strong black mind.* When I got upset because my *J-5 'fro* wouldn't stay up like the other kids at school (smile), it was her that told me to get the dictionary from the foyer closet, so I could discover the *one-drop rule.* It was her that had me read and sketch from my father's *'67 Negro Almanac.* And it was she, along with my father, who framed my mindset to belief that all people had been blessed with the ability to reason. Those, whose love for others was ignorant to race, creed, and color, were thankful. Those who discriminated without regard for character were not grateful for what God had given.

Along with her passing in 2014 on February 1, came the realization that annually, the first day of Black History Month would forever mark that event for me. To this point, there is no recent *Yager* off-spring to carry on our name from the maternal side, as most of my cousins (female) have taken the sole names of their spouses. Authoring this project as such has assured me that her legacy will live on, and be celebrated in the cultural spirit for which she lived.

Dr. A. Yager Wyatt
2.1.2015

End Notes

Core References

AAPC. (2014a). About AAPC. Retrieved from the AAPC website: https://www.aapc.com/AboutUs/

AAPC. (2014b). Medical Auditing. Retrieved from the AAPC website: https://www.aapc.com/medical-auditing/medical-auditing.aspx

Aggelidis, V. P., & Chatzoglou, P. D. (2008). Methods for evaluating hospital information systems: A literature re view. *EuroMed Journal of Business,3*(1), 99-118. Re trieved from http://www.emeraldinsight.com/doi/abs/10.1108/1450219 0810873849

American Cancer Society. (2014). Home. Retrieved from the American Cancer Society website: http://www.cancer.org/

American College of Healthcare Executives (2011, November

11). Code of Ethics. Retrieved from the ACHE website: http://www.ache.org/abt_ache/code.cfm

American College of Healthcare Executives. (2012, March). Statement on Diversity. Retrieved from the ACHE web site: http://www.ache.org/policy/diversity.cfm

American College of Healthcare Executives. (2013). Ethics toolkit. Retrieved from the ACHE website: http://www.ache.org/ABT_ACHE/EthicsToolkit/UsingCode.cfm

American Dental Association. (2014). ADA Center for Informatics and Standards. Retrieved from the ADA website: http://www.ada.org/en/member-center/member-benefits/practice-resources/dental-informatics

American Health Information Management Association. (2007). Statement on Quality Healthcare and Information. American Health Information Management Association. Retrieved from

Afroinformatics™

http://library.ahima.org/xpedio/groups/public/documents/ahima/bok1_047492.pdf

American Health Information Management Association.(2008, November). Statement on Data Stewardship. *American Health Information Management Association*. Retrieved from http://library.ahima.org/xpedio/groups/public/documents/ahima/bok1_047418.hcsp?dDocName=bok1_047418

Amatayakul, M. (2008). Good data stewardship makes good cents. *Healthcare Financial Management, 62*(2), 122–124.Retrieved from http://www.ncbi.nlm.nih.gov/pubmed/18309603

American Medical Association. (2008, July 30). The AMA's role in U.S. health care. Retrieved from the AMA web site: http://www.ama-assn.org/ama/pub/news/speeches/ama-role-us-healthcare.page

Angelopoulos, C., Thomas, S., Hechler, S., Parissis, N., & Hlavacek, M. (2008, Oct). Comparisons between digi tal panoramic radiology and cone-beam computed to mography for the identification of the mandibular ca nal as part of presurgical dental implant assessment. *Journal of Oral and Maxillofacial Surgery, Vol, 66*(10) pp. 2130-2135. Retrieved from http://www.ncbi.nlm.nih.gov/pubmed/18848113

Aquil, A., Lippeveld, T., & Hozumi, D. (2009). PRISM framework: a paradigm shift for designing, strengthen ing and evaluating routine health information systems, *Health Policy Plan, 24*(3). 217-228. Retrieved from http://www.ncbi.nlm.nih.gov/pmc/articles/PMC267097 6/pdf/czp010.pdf

Arizona State University. (2014). School of Computing, Informatics, & Decision Systems Engineering. Re trieved from the ASU Ira A. Fulton School of Engi

neering website:

http://cidse.engineering.asu.edu/forstudent/prospective

-students/computer-systems-engineering/

Aragon, S., Richardson, L., Lawrence, W., & Gesell, S.

(2013). Nurses' patient-centeredness and perceptions of

care among Medicaid patients in hospital obstetrical

units. Nurs Res Pract. 2013; 2013: 563282. Retrieved

from

http://www.ncbi.nlm.nih.gov/pmc/articles/PMC376214

1/pdf/NRP2013-563282.pdf

Arlotto, P. W., Birch, P. C., Crockett, M. H., & Irby, S. P.

(2007). *Beyond return on investment:Expanding the val

ue of healthcare information technology.* Chicago, IL:

Healthcare Information and Management Systems Socie

ty

Arraj, V. (2013). ITIL®: the basics whitepaper. Retrieved from

End Notes

https://www.axelos.com/CMSPages/GetFile.aspx?guid=
6117a138-b873-43b9-9fea-372bf6b26bfe

Aspinall, M., & Hamermesh, R. (2007). Realizing the promise
of personalized medicine. *Harvard Business Re*
view,85(10), 108–117. Retrieved from
http://www.researchgate.net/publication/5872873_Real
izing_the_promise_of_personalized_medicine

AXELOS. (2014). Introducing ITIL®-The world's most
widely used service management framework. Re
trieved from
https://www.axelos.com/Corporate/media/Files/Brochu
res/ITIL_Product_Brochure_Conference_Version_v1.p
df

Barr, F. (2010). Nursing peer review: Raising the bar on
quality. *American Nursing Today, 5*(9), 46-48. Re
trieved from
http://www.americannursetoday.com/assets/0/434/436/

Afroinformatics™

440/6850/7034/7050/7078/29bd2042-4501-4037-a200-cfdde5b8e53f.pdf

Barton, P. (2010). *Understanding the U.S. health services system.* (4 ed.). Chicago: Health Administration Press.

Bassi, J., & Lau, F. (2013). Measuring value for money: a scoping review on economic evaluation of health in formation systems, *J Am Med Inform Assoc, 20*(4), 792-801. Retrieved from http://www.ncbi.nlm.nih.gov/pmc/articles/PMC372116 2/pdf/amiajnl-2012-001422.pdf

Bergrath, S., Rossaint, R., Lenssen, N., Fitzner, C., and Skorning, M. (2013). Prehospital digital photography and automated image transmission in an emergency medical service – an ancillary retrospective analysis of a prospective controlled trial. *Scand J Trauma Resusc Emerg Med., 21*(3). Retrieved from http://www.ncbi.nlm.nih.gov/pmc/articles/PMC356801 6/pdf/1757-7241-21-3.pdf

Bernard, D., Cowan, C., Selden, T., Cai, L., & Heffler, S. (2012). Reconciling medical expenditure estimates from the MEPS and NHEA, 2007. *Medicare & Medi caid Research Review, Vol, 2*(4), E1-E20. Retrieved from http://dx.doi.org/10.5600/mmrr.002.04.a09

Bland, R. L. (2015). Financial incentives for HIT adoption (A. Wyatt, Interviewer). Rodney L. Bland, D.P.M., Frank lin, VA. southamptonfoot@gmail.com

Bloomrosen, M., and Detmer, D. (2010). Informatics, evidence-based care, and research; implications for national poli cy: a report of an American Medical Informatics Associ ation health policy conference, *J Am Med Inform Assoc,17*(2), 115-123. Retrieved from http://www.ncbi.nlm.nih.gov/pmc/articles/PMC3000781/pdf/jamia001370.pdf

Borkowski, N. (2009). *Organizational behavior, theory, and design in health care.* Sudbury, MA: Jones and Bartlett Publishers.

Borycki, E., Kushniruk, A., & Carvalho, C. (2013). Methodol

ogy for Validating Safety Heuristics Using Clinical

Simulations: Identifying and Preventing Possible

Technology-Induced Errors Related to Using Health

Information Systems, *Comput Math Methods*

Med, Published online. Retrieved from

http://www.ncbi.nlm.nih.gov/pmc/articles/PMC362632

2/pdf/CMMM2013-526419.pdf

Buchbinder, S. B., & Shanks, N. H. (Eds.). (2012).

Introducion to health care management (2nded.). Bur

lington, MA: Jones & Bartlett Learning.

Bureau of Labor Statistics. (2014a). Medical Records and

Health Information Technicians. Retrieved November

13, 2014 from the

Bureau of Labor Statistics website:

http://www.bls.gov/ooh/healthcare/medical-records-

and-health-information-technicians.htm

Bureau of Labor Statistics. (2014b). Medical and Health Ser

vices Managers. Retrieved November 13, 2014 from the

Bureau of Labor Statistics website:

http://www.bls.gov/ooh/management/medical-and-

health-services-managers.htm

Burton, T. M. (2009, October 8). News in Depth: U.S. hospitals

find way to make care cheaper—Make it better—

Publishing outcomes can boost results, one state discov

ers. *Wall Street Journal* (Europe), p. 14. Retrieved from

http://academicguides.waldenu.edu/mmba6693

Carlbrashear Dot Org. (2014). Home. Retrieved from the Carl

Brashear.org website: http://www.carlbrashear.org/

Centers for Advanced Forensics. (2014). QSNP Forensic

Informatics. Retrieved from the Centers for Advanced

Forensics website:

http://www.advanced-forensics.com/technology/

Centers for Disease Control and Prevention. (2009). Compe

tencies for public health informatics. Retrieved from

http://www.cdc.gov//InformaticsCompetencies/downlo

ads/PHI_Competencies.pdf

Centers for Disease Control and Prevention. (2010). Address

ing High Infant Mortality Rates Among African Amer

icans. Retrieved from

http://www.cdc.gov/washington/~cdcatWork/pdf/infan

t_mortality.pdf

Centers for Disease Control and Prevention. (2013, June 19).

ICD and ICF home. Retrieved from the CDC website:

http://www.cdc.gov/nchs/icd.htm

Centers for Disease Control and Prevention. (2014a). BRFSS

prevalence and trends data, 2013. Retrieved from the

CDC website:

http://apps.nccd.cdc.gov/brfss/page.asp?cat=CV&yr=2

013&state=All#CV

Centers for Disease Control and Prevention. (2014b). Black or

African American Populations. Retrieved from the

CDC website:

http://www.cdc.gov/minorityhealth/populations/remp/b

lack.html

Centers for Disease Control. (2014c). Enterovirus D68 in the United States, 2014. Retrieved from the CDC web site: http://www.cdc.gov/non-polio-enterovirus/about/EV-D68.html

Centers for Disease Control and Prevention. (2014d). Global Public Health Informatics Program. Retrieved from the CDC website: http://www.cdc.gov/globalhealth/healthprotection/ghsb/gphi/default.htm

Centers for Disease Control and Prevention and University of Washington's Center for Public Health Informatics. Competencies for Public Health Informatics. Atlanta, GA: US Department of Health and Human Services, Centers for Disease Control and Prevention. (2009). Retrieved from http://www.cdc.gov/InformaticsCompetencies

Centers for Medicare & Medicaid Services. (n.d.). Research,

statistics, data, & systems. Retrieved from the CMS

website: https://www.cms.gov/Research-Statistics-

Data-and-Systems/Research-Statistics-Data-and-

Systems.html

Chappell, K. (2006). America's wealthiest black country.

Ebony, 62(1). Retrieved from

http://books.google.com/books?id=y83g7W0jFPQC&p

rintsec=frontcover&rview=1#v=onepage&q&f=false

Chen, J., Ou, L., & Hollis, S. (2013). A systematic review of

the impact of routine collection of patient reported out

come measures on patients, providers and health or

ganizations in an oncologic setting. BMC Health Serv

Res. 2013; 13: 211. Retrieved from

http://www.biomedcentral.com/1472-6963/13/211

Chernew, M. (2010). Bundled payment systems: Can they be

more successful this time? *Health Services Research,*

45(5, Part 1), 1141–1147. Retrieved from

http://www.ncbi.nlm.nih.gov/pmc/articles/PMC2965497/

pdf/hesr0045-1141.pdf

Clancy, C. (2009). Testimony: March 18, 2009. Department of
Health and Human Services. Retrieved from
http://www.hhs.gov/asl/testify/2009/03/t20090318b.ht
ml

Cisco, Inc. (2014). Products & Services. Retrieved from the
Cisco, Inc. website:
http://www.cisco.com/c/en/us/products/index.html

Cliff, B. (2012). Using technology to enhance patient-centered
care. *Journal of HealthcareManagement, 57*(5), 301-3.
Retrieved from
http://www.ache.org/PUBS/JHM/57-5/57-
5_Cliff_PCC.pdf

Coder Fitzgerald, R. (1979). A Different Story: A Black
History of Fredericksburg, Stafford, and Spotsylvania,
Virginia. [Fredericksburg, VA]: Unicorn

Collins, J., & Weiner, S. (2010). Proposal for the creation of a
subdiscipline: Education informatics. Teachers College

Record 112, no. 10: 2523-2536. Retrieved from

http://dash.harvard.edu/handle/1/4569474

Columbia University. (2014). Department of Biomedical

Informatics (DBMI). Retrieved from the Columbia

University DBMI website:

https://www.dbmi.columbia.edu/

Columbia University Mailman School of Public Health.

(2014). Department: Epidemiology Certificate: Public

Health Informatics. Retrieved from

http://www.mailman.columbia.edu/sites/default/files/5

%20COPIES%20-

%20Public%20Health%20Informatics%20-

%20EPI.pdf

Committee on Quality of Health Care in America, & Institute

of Medicine. (2001). *Crossing the quality chasm: A

new health system for the 21ˢᵗ century.* Washington, D.

C.: National Academy Press.

Cruchaga, C., et al. (2013). Rare coding variants in the phos pholipase D3 gene confer risk for Alzheimer's disease.

Nature , published online Dec. 11. Retrieved from

http://www.nia.nih.gov/alzheimers/announcements/201

4/01/rare-genetic-variants-may-double-risk-

alzheimers-disease

Cruise, M. (2014, December 20). Competencies. (A. Wyatt,

Interviewer). melanicruise@yahoo.com

Cummings, G., Spiers, J., Sharlow, J., Germann, P.,

Yurtseven, O., & Bhatti, A. (2013). Worklife im

provement and leadership development study: A learn

ing experience in leadership development and

"planned" organizational change. *Health Care Man

agement Review, 38*(1), 81-93. Retrieved from

http://www.ncbi.nlm.nih.gov/pubmed/22314974

Daily Press. (2005). Medical School Bridge: Striving For

Students' Success. (KYM KLASS special to Daily

Press). Retrieved from

http://articles.dailypress.com/2005-05-

Afroinformatics™

05/news/0505050040_1_professional-schools-dental-schools-mcat

Dandara, D., Adebamowo, C., de Vries, J., Dove, E., Fisher, E., Gibbs, R., Hotez, P., Kickbusch, I Knoppers,B., Masellis, M., Milius, Oestergaard, M., Pang, T., & Rotimi, C. (2012). An idea whose time has come? An African foresight observatory on genomics medicine and data-intensive global scienc. *Current Pharmaceu tical and Personalized Medicine, 10*(1), 7-15 2770–2777. Retrieved from http://www.benthamdirect.org/pages/content.php?CPP M/2012/00000010/00000001/002AF.SGM

Das, A., Schwartz, J., & DeRenzo, E. G. (2003). True risk management: Physician's liability risk and the practice of patient-centered medicine. *Journal of Law and Health, 18*(1), 57–69. Retrieved from http://engagedscholarship.csuohio.edu/cgi/viewcontent.cg i?article=1115&context=jlh

End Notes

Dawkins, E., Michimi, A., Ellis-Griffith, G., Peterson, T., Carter, D., & English, G. (2013). Dental caries among children visiting a mobile dental clinic in South Central Kentucky: a pooled cross-sectional study. *BMC Oral Health 13*(19). Retrieved from http://www.ncbi.nlm.nih.gov/pubmed/23639250

DeLia, D., Hoover, D., & Cantor, J. (2012). Statistical uncertainty in the medicare shared savings program. *Medicare & Medicaid Research Review, Vol, 2*(4), E1-E16. Retrieved from http://www.cms.gov/mmrr/Downloads/MMRR2012_0 02_04_a04.pdf

Detmer, D., Benson, M., & Lehmann, C. (2010). Clinical informatics board certification: History, current status, and predicted impact on the clinical informatics workforce. *Applclin Inform, 1*(1), 11-18. Retrieved from http://www.ncbi.nlm.nih.gov/pmc/articles/PMC3631890/ pdf/ACI-01-0011.pdf

DiMatteo, A. (n.d.). Shaping dentistry with CAD/CAM

technology. Retrieved from:

http://www.yourdentistryguide.com/cad-cam-tech/

Diop, Cheikh Anta (1989-07-01). The African Origin of

Civilization: Myth or Reality (p. 53). Chicago Review

Press. Kindle Edition.

Dolin, R., & Alschuler, L. (2010, August). Approaching

semantic interoperability in health level seven. *Journal*

of American Informatics Association, 18, 99-103.

Retrieved from

http://www.ncbi.nlm.nih.gov/pmc/articles/PMC300587

8/pdf/amiajnl7864.pdf

Dougherty, M. (2006). Long-term care's IT agenda: Industry

summit produces 11 action items for health IT adop

tion. *Journal of AHIMA* 77(1), 64-65. Retrieved from

http://library.ahima.org/xpedio/groups/public/documen

ts/ahima/bok1_028982.hcsp?dDocName=bok1_02898

2

Dye, B., Li, X., & Thornton-Evans, G. (2012). Oral health disparities as determined by selected Healthy People 2020 Oral Health Objectives for the United States, 2009-2010. *NCHS Data Brief*, No. 104. Retrieved from http://www.cdc.gov/nchs/data/databriefs/db104.pdf

Education Portal. (2014). Information systems, operations manager, informatics[search]. Retrieved from the Edu cation Portal web site: http://education-portal.com

Elizabeth Glaser Pediatric Aids Foundation. (2012, July 22). Statement on the importance of community based or ganizations in pediatric HIV/AIDS fight. Retrieved from http://egpaf-ias.org/2012/07/22/statement-on-the-importance-of-community-based-organizations-in-pediatric-hivaids-fight/

Englebardt, S. P., & Nelson, R. (2002). *Health care informatics: An interdisciplinary approach.* St. Louis: Mosby.

Eskelin, A. (2001). *Technology acquisition: Buying the future of your business*. Upper Saddle River, NJ: Addison-Wesley/Pearson Education.

Fox, M. L. (2006). Job design. *Encyclopedia of career devel opment*. Thousand Oaks, CA: Sage.

Freshman, B., & Rubino, L. (2002). Emotional intelligence: A core competency for health care administrators. *Health Care Manager, 20(4)*, 1–9. Retrieved from http://www.ncbi.nlm.nih.gov/pubmed/12083173

Friedman, L. (2014, Jan 9). Huge racial gap in life expectancy. Business Insider. Retrieved from http://www.businessinsider.com/huge-racial-gap-in-life-expectancy-2014-1

Friedman, M., Schueth, A., Bell, D. (2009, March). Interoper able electronic prescribing in the United States: A pro gress report. *Health Affairs, 28*(2), 393-403. Retrieved from http://content.healthaffairs.org/content/28/2/393.full

Franklin, M. A., Mapes, D., McDow, A., & Mithamo, K.

(2012). The merger of two competing hospitals – Case for chapters 5, 2, and 12. In Buchbinder, S. B., & Shanks, N. H., *Introduction to health care manage ment* (2nd ed., p. 406-411). Burlington, MA: Jones & Bartlett Learning.

Fryer, R., & Greenstone, M. (2007). The causes and consequenc es of attending historically black colleges and universi ties. *American Economic Journal: Applied Economics, 2*(1),116-48. Retrieved from http://www.nber.org/papers/w13036

Gackowski, A., Czekierda, L., Chrustowicz, A., Cała, J., Nowak, M., Sadowski, J., Podolec, P., Pasowicz, M., and Zieliński, K. (2011). Development, implementa tion, and multicenter clinical validation of the TeleDICOM—advanced, interactive teleconsultation system. *J Digit Imaging. June; 24*(3): 541–551. Re trieved from http://www.ncbi.nlm.nih.gov/pmc/articles/PMC309205

1/pdf/10278_2010_Article_9303. pdf

Galt, K. A., & Paschal, K. A. (2011). *Foundations in patient safety for health professionals.* Sudbury, MA: Jones & Bartlett.

George Mason University. (1971). Virginia State Advisory Committee to the U.S. Commission on Civil Rights: Press advisor. Retrieved from http://ahistoryofmason.gmu.edu/archive/files/7ea9d9c6 60c5ea03ebb233529abdbcde.pdf

Giannangelo, K. (2010). *Healthcare code sets, clinical termi nologies, and classification systems* (2nd ed.). Chica go: American Health Information Management Asso ciation.

Glaser, J. (2006). IT proposals competing for attention? Learn how to prioritize. *hfm (Healthcare Financial Manage ment)*, *60*(7), 92–96. Retrieved from http://connection.ebscohost.com/c/articles/21545582/pro

posals-competing-attention-learn-how-prioritize

Glaser, J. (2009). Strategies for ensuring an IT project delivers value. *Healthcare Financial Management, 63*(7), 28-31. Retrieved from http://www.unboundmedicine.com/medline/citation/1958 8807/Strategies_for_ensuring_an_IT_project_delivers_v alue_

Goldsmith, J. (2011). Accountable care organizations: The case for flexible partnerships between health plans and pro viders. *Health Affairs, 30*(1), 32-40. Retrieved from http://www.healthfutures.net/pdf/Accountable_Care_Org anizations.pdf

Goodwin, S., & Anderson, G. (2012). Effect of cost-sharing reductions on preventive service use among medicare fee-for-service beneficiaries. *Medicare & Medicaid Research Review, Vol, 2*(1), E1-E26. Retrieved from http://www.healthfutures.net/pdf/Accountable_Care_O rganizations.pdf

González, D., Carpenter, T., van Hemert, J., & Wardlaw, J.

(2010). An open source toolkit for medical imaging de-

identification. *European Radiology, 20* (8), p1896-

1904.9p. Retrieved from

http://link.springer.com/article/10.1007%2Fs00330-

010-1745-3

Grinnell Regional Medical Center. (2013). About us. Re

trieved March 30, 2013, from

http://www.grmc.us/about-us

Guéant, J., Guéant-Rodriguez, R., Gastin, I., Cornejo-García,

J., Viola, M., Barbaud, A., Mertes P., Blanca, M., Ro

mano, A. (2008). Pharmacogenetic determinants of

immediate and delayed reactions of drug hypersensi

tivity. *Current Pharmaceutical Design, 14*(27), 2770–

2777. Retrieved from

http://www.pharmigene.com/en/studies-

publications/Publications-A05-2008.html

Gurwitz, J., Field, T., Rochon, P., Judge, J., Harrold, L., Bell,

C., Lee, M., White, K., LaPrino, J., Erramuspe-Mainard, J., DeFlorio, M., Gavendo, L., Barill, J., Reed, G., & Bates, D. (2008, Dec). Effect of computer ized provider order entry with clinical decision support on adverse drug events in the long-term care setting. *Journal of the American Geriatrics Society, 56* (12), p2225-2233. Retrieved from http://www.ncbi.nlm.nih.gov/pubmed/19093922

Gwinnett Technical College. (2014). Health Information Technology (HIT) Certificate Program. Retrieved from the Gwinnett Technical College website: http://www.gwinnetttech.edu/HIT

Handfield-Jones, R., & Kocha, W. (1999, Feb.).The role of medical organizations in supporting doctor-patient communication. *Cancer Prevention Control, Vol, 3*(1), pp 46-50. Retrieved from http://www.ncbi.nlm.nih.gov/pubmed/10474752

Harvard Medical School. (2014). Translational Informatics.

Afroinformatics™

Center for Biomedical Informatics. Retrieved from the

Harvard Medical School CBMI website:

https://cbmi.med.harvard.edu/research/translational-

informatics

Hawkes, J & Marsh, W. (2004). Discovering statistics.

Charleston, South Carolina: Quant Systems, Inc.

Healthcare Information and Management Systems Society.

(2014). What is Nursing Informatics? Retrieved from

the HiMSS website:

http://www.himss.org/resourcelibrary/TopicList.aspx?

MetaDataID=767

Health Information Exchange Steering Committee. (2009).

Overview of Health Information Exchange (HIE),

Health Information and Management Systems Society

(HiMSS). Retrieved from

http://www.himss.org/files/HIMSSorg/content/files/R

HIO/RHIO_HIE_GeneralPresentation.pdf

HealthIT Dot Gov. (2014). Nationwide Health Information

Network (NwHIN). Retrieved from the HealthIT.gov

web site: http://www.healthit.gov/policy-researchers-

implementers/nationwide-health-information-network-

nwhin

Health Level Seven. (2014). About. Retrieved from the HL7

website: http://www.hl7.org/about/index.cfm?ref=nav

Health Research Institute. (2014). Medical cost trend: Behind

the numbers 2015. Health Research Institute. Re

trieved from the PwC's Health Research Insti

tute website: http://www.pwc.com/us/medicalcosttrend

Hebda, T., & Czar, P., (2013). *Handbook of Informatics for*

Nurses & Healthcare Professionals.

New Jersey: Pearson Education.

Hefner, D., & Malcolm, C. (2002). 15 essential steps of IT

project management. *HealthcareFinancial Management*,

56(2), 76-78. Retrieved from

http://www.unboundmedicine.com/medline/citation/1184

2507/15_essential_steps_of_IT_project_management_

Held, G. (n.d.). 50-30-19 Windows NT Architecture, *IT Today*. Retrieved from http://www.ittoday.info/AIMS/DCM/50-30-19.pdf

Hernandez, P., Schultz, P., Estrada, M., Woodcock, A., & Chance, R. (2013). Sustaining optimal motivation: A longitudinal analysis of interventions to broaden par ticipation of underrepresented students in STEM . *J Educ Psychol, 105*(1). Retrieved from http://www.ncbi.nlm.nih.gov/pmc/articles/PMC383841 1/pdf/nihms512414.pdf

Hersh, W. (2010). The health information technology work force: Estimations of demands and a framework for re quirements, *Appl Clin Inform, 1*(2), 197-212. Retrieved from http://www.ncbi.nlm.nih.gov/pmc/articles/PMC363227 9/pdf/ACI-01-0197.pdf

Hersh, W., & Wright, A. (2010). What workforce is needed to implement the health information technology agenda?

End Notes

Analysis from the HIMSS Analytics™ Database,

AMIA Annu Symp Pro, 2008, 303–307. Retrieved from

http://www.ncbi.nlm.nih.gov/pmc/articles/PMC265603

3/pdf/amia-0303-s2008.pdf

Hildreth, S. (2007). Making it real: How companies get

started on ITIL. *Computerworld,* 41(48), 34-38. Re

trieved from

http://www.computerworld.com/article/2552446/it-

management/making-it-real.html

Hincapie, A., Warholak, T., Murcko, A., Slack, M., & Malone,

D. (2011). Physicians' opinions of a health information

exchange, *J Am Med Inform Assoc,* 18(1), 60-65. Re

trieved from

http://www.ncbi.nlm.nih.gov/pmc/articles/PMC3005874/

pdf/amiajnl6502.pdf

HIPAA Academy. (2014). About HIPAA Certification Online.

Retrieved from the HIPAA Academy website:

http://www.hipaacertificationonline.com/CSCS.html

Hodge, J. G., Jr., Gostin, L. O., & Jacobson, P. D. (1999). Legal issues concerning electronic health information: Privacy, quality, and liability. *JAMA: Journal of the American Medical Association, 282*(15), 1466–1471. Retrieved from http://jama.jamanetwork.com/article.aspx?articleid=1920 04

Holmes, T. (2005, Aug 1). Blacks underrepresented in legal field. Retrieved from Black Enterprise web site: http://www.blackenterprise.com/mag/blacks-underrepresented-in-legal-field/

Howell, T. (2006, April 18). Census 2000 Special Report. Maryland Newsline, Census: Md. Economy Supports Black-Owned Businesses. University of Maryland, Philip Merrill College of Journalism. Retrieved from http://www.newsline.umd.edu/business/specialreports/ census/blackbusiness041806.htm

Hurd, N., Sánchez, B., Zimmerman, M., & Caldwell, C.

(2013). Natural Mentors, Racial Identity, and Educational Attainment among African American Adolescents: Exploring Pathways to Success, Child Dev, 83(4), 1196-1212. Retrieved from http://www.ncbi.nlm.nih.gov/pmc/articles/PMC3399968/pdf/nihms362593.pdf

Information Technology Infrastructure Library. (2013a). Home. Retrieved from the ITIL web site: http://www.itil-officialsite.com/

Information Technology Infrastructure Library. (2013b). ITIL Service Management. Retrieved June 01, 2013, from the ITIL website: https://www.axelos.com/best-practice-solutions

Institute of Medicine. (1999). *To err is human.* Washington, DC: National Academy of Sciences. Retrieved from https://www.iom.edu/~/media/Files/Report%20Files/1999/To-Err-is-Hu

Afroinformatics™

man/To%20Err%20is%20Human%201999%20%20repo

rt%20brief.pdf

Institute of Medicine. (2001). *Crossing the quality chasm: A*

new health system for the 21st century. Washington, DC:

National Academy of Sciences. Retrieved from

http://www.iom.edu/Reports/2001/Crossing-the-Quality-

Chasm-A-New-Health-System-for-the-21st-

Century.aspx

Institute of Medicine. (2014). Crossing the Quality Chasm:

The IOM Health Care Quality Initiative. Retrieved

online from

http://www.iom.edu/Global/News%20Announcements

/Crossing-the-Quality-Chasm-The-IOM-Health-Care-

Quality-Initiative.aspx

Institute of Training Science and Sports Informatics. (2006).

Technology enables university intellectual capital

management, Computerworld Honors Program [case

study]. Retrieved from

End Notes

http://www.cwhonors.org/case_studies/InstituteofTrain

ingScience.pdf

International Conference on Ecological Informatics. (2014).

Conference Theme: Ecological Informatics for Envi

ronmental Sustainability. About. Retrieved from the

ICEI website:

http://www.icei2014.org/about/themes.html

International Medical Informatics Association. (2014). Prima

ry Health Care Informatics. Retrieved from the IMIA

website: http://www.imia-medinfo.org/new2/node/149

International Organization for Standardization. (2013). About

Us. Retrieved from the Internation

al Organization for Standardization website:

http://www.iso.org/iso/home/about.htm

Internet Movie Database. (n.d.). Men of Honor. Retrieved

from the IMDB web site:

http://www.imdb.com/title/tt0203019/

James, R., Starks, H., Segrest, V., & Burke, W. (2012). From leaky pipeline to irrigation system: minority education

through the lens of community-based participatory re

search, *Prog Community Health Partnersh, 6*(4), 471-

479. Retrieved from

http://www.ncbi.nlm.nih.gov/pmc/articles/PMC395138

2/pdf/nihms554110.pdf

Jelliffe, W., Bayard, D., Schumitzky, A., Milman, M., & Van

Guilder, M. (1994). Pharmaco-informatics: more pre

cise drug therapy from "multiple model" (MMI) sto

chastic adaptive control regimens: evaluation with

simulated vancomycin therapy. *Proc Annu Symp*

Comput Appl Med Care, 972. Retrieved from

http://www.ncbi.nlm.nih.gov/pmc/articles/PMC224780

6/pdf/procascamc00001-0934.pdf

Johnson, N., Murphy, A., McNeese, N., Reddy, M., & Purao,

S. (2013). A Survey of Rural Hospitals' Perspectives

on Health Information Technology Outsourcing. *AMIA*

Annu Symp Proc, 732-741. Retrieved from

http://www.ncbi.nlm.nih.gov/pmc/articles/PMC379755
2/pdf/phim0010-0001e.pdf

Johns Hopkins Bloomberg School of Public Health. (2014).
What Is Public Health Informatics? Retrieved from the
Johns Hopkins Bloomberg School of Public Health web
site: http://www.jhsph.edu/departments/health-policy-
and-management/certificates/public-health-
informatics/what-is-health-informatics.html

Joint Commission. (2010). Patient Safety. *The Joint Commission
SentinelEvent Alert, 48*:1-4. Retrieved from
http://www.jointcommission.org/assets/1/18/SEA_48.pdf

Joint Commission. (2013, April 8). Medical device safety in
hospitals. *The Joint Commission Sentinel Event Alert,
50*:1-3. Retrieved from
http://www.jointcommission.org/assets/1/18/SEA_50_ala
rms_4_5_13_FINAL1.PDF

Joshi, A., Puricelli Perin, D. M. (2012). Gaps in the existing
public health informatics training programs: A challenge

to the development of a skilled global workforce.

Perspect Health Inf Manag, 9(Fall), 11-18. Retrieved

from

http://www.ncbi.nlm.nih.gov/pmc/articles/PMC3510646/

pdf/phim0009-0001c.pdf

Journal of Blacks in Higher Education. (2014). More

Than 4.5 Million African Americans Now Hold a

Four-Year College Degree. JBHE: News & Views. Re

trieved November 13, 2014 from the JBHE website:

http://www.jbhe.com/news_views/64_degrees.html

Journal of Education, Informatics and Cybernetics. (2014).

Home. Retrieved from the Journal of Education, In

formatics and Cybernetics website:

http://www.iiisci.org/journal/sci/Home.asp

Kagawa-Singer, M., & Blackhall, L. J. (2001). Negotiating

cross-cultural issues at the end of life: "You got to go

where he lives." *JAMA: Journal of the American Medi

cal Association, 286*(23), 2993–3001. Retrieved from

http://www.ncbi.nlm.nih.gov/pubmed/11743841

Kaipa, P. (2000). Knowledge architecture for the twenty-first century. *Behaviour & Information Technology, 19*(3), 153–161.Retrieved from http://www.researchgate.net/publication/247494897_K nowledge_architecture_for_the_twenty-first_century

Kaiser Commission on Medicaid and the Uninsured. (2014). Key facts about the uninsured population. Retrieved from http://files.kff.org/attachment/key-facts-about-the-uninsured-population-fact-sheet

Kampov-Polevoi, J., & Hemminger, B. (2011). A curricula-based comparison of biomedical and health informatics pro grams in the USA. *J Am Med Inform Assoc, 18*(2), 195-202. Retrieved from http://www.ncbi.nlm.nih.gov/pmc/articles/PMC3116256/ #supplementary-material-sec

Kaushal, R., Jha, A., Franz, C., Glaser, J., Shetty, K., Jaggi, T., Middelton, B., Kuperman, G., Khoransani, R.,

Tanasijevic, M., Bates, D., & Brigham and Women's Hospital CPOE Working Group. (2006). Return on investment for a computerized physician order system. *Journal of the American Medical Informatics Association, 13*(3), 261–266. Retrieved from http://www.ncbi.nlm.nih.gov/pmc/articles/PMC1513660/pdf/261.pdf

Kawamoto, K., Lobach, D., Willard, H., & Ginsburg, G. (2009). A national clinical decision support infrastructure to enable the widespread and consistent practice of genomic and personalized medicine. *BMC Medical Informatics & Decision Making, 9*, 1–14. Retrieved from http://www.healthpolicyandtechnology.org/article/S2211-8837(12)00038-X/references

Keeppanasseril, A., Matthew, A., Muddappa, S. (2011). Effectiveness of tele-guided interceptive prosthodontic treatment in rural India: A comparative pilot study. *OnlineJournal of Public Health Informatics, 3*(2) Re trieved from:

http://www.ncbi.nlm.nih.gov/pubmed/23569611

Kotter, J. P. (1999). What leaders really do. Boston: Harvard

Business School Press.

Kotter, J. P. (2007, January). Leading change: Why transfor

mation efforts fail. *Harvard Business Review,85*(1),

96–103. Retrieved from

https://hbr.org/2007/01/leading-change-why-

transformation-efforts-fail/ar/1

Krause, D., May, W., & Cossman, J. (2012). Overcoming data

challenges examining oral health disparities in Appala

chia. *Online Journal of Public Health Informatics, Vol,*

4(3) Retrieved from:

http://ojphi.org/article/viewFile/4279/3390

Kreuter, M., Griffith, D., Thompson, V., Brownson, R.,

McClure, S., Scharff, D., Clark, E., & Haire-Joshu, D.

(2011). Lessons learned from a decade of focused re

cruitment and training to develop minority public

health professionals, *Am J Public Health, 101*(Suppl

1), S188–S195. Retrieved from

http://www.ncbi.nlm.nih.gov/pmc/articles/PMC322248

1/pdf/S188.pdf

Kropf, R., & Scalzi, G. (2008). Great project management = IT

success. *Physician Executive, 34*(3), 38-40. Retrieved

from http://www.ncbi.nlm.nih.gov/pubmed/18605270

Lane, S. G., Longstreth, E., & Nixon, V. (2001). A community

leader's guide to hospital finance: Evaluating how a hos

pital gets and spends its money. *Harvard School of

Publich Health: The Access Project*, 1-45. Retrieved from

http://accessproject.org/a_community_leaders_guide_to_

hospital_finance.pdf

Lang, A. (2014). Government capacities and stakeholders:

what facilitates ehealth legislation? *Global Health,

10*(4). Retrieved from

http://www.ncbi.nlm.nih.gov/pmc/articles/PMC392544

5/pdf/1744-8603-10-4.pdf

Leatherman, S., Berwick, D., Iles, D., Lewin, L., Davidoff, F.,

  Nolan, T., & Bisognano, M. (2003). The business case

  for quality: Case studies and an analysis. *Health Affairs,*

  22(2), 17–30. Retrieved from

  http://content.healthaffairs.org/content/22/2/17.full.pdf+h

  tml

Liberal arts. (n.d.). In Merriam-Webster's online dictionary.

  Retrieved from http://www.merriam-

  webster.com/concise/liberal%20arts

Longo, D. R., Hewitt, J. E., Ge, B., & Schubert, S. (2007).

  Hospital patient safety: Characteristics of best-

  performing hospitals. *Journal of Healthcare Manage*

  ment, 52(3), 188–205. Retrieved from

  http://www.ncbi.nlm.nih.gov/pubmed/17552355

Love, T., Cebul, R., Einstadter, D., Jain, A., Miller, H., Harris,

  C., Greco, P., Husak, S., Dawson, N. (2008, Apr).

  Electronic medical record-assisted design of a cluster-

  randomized trial to improve diabetes care and out

comes. *JGIM: Journal of General Internal Medicine, 23*(4), p383-391. 9p. Retrieved from http://www.ncbi.nlm.nih.gov/pubmed/17552355

MacTaggart, P., & Hyatt Thorpe, J. (2013). Long-term care and health information technology: Opportunities and responsibilities for long-term and post-acute care providers. *Perspect Health Inf Manag, 1e*. Retrieved from http://www.ncbi.nlm.nih.gov/pmc/articles/PMC3797552/pdf/phim0010-0001e.pdf

Mack, J., Paulk, E., Viswanath, K., & Prigerson, H. (2010). Black-white disparities in the effects of communication on medical care received near death. Arch Intern Med.2010 September 27; 170(17): 1533–1540. Retrieved from http://www.ncbi.nlm.nih.gov/pmc/articles/PMC3739279/pdf/nihms491694.pdf

Manning, K. (1983). Black Apollo of Science: The Life of

End Notes

Ernest Everett Just (Kindle Location1). Kindle Edition.

Marchibroda, J. (2004). The Role of Community Health Infrastructures and a National HealthInformation Infra structure in Quality Enhancement [Power Point Presentation]. Retrieved online from http://www.powershow.com/view1/1b7306-ZDc1Z/The_Role_of_Community_Health_Infrastructu res_and_a_National_Health_Information_Infrastructur e_in_Quality_Enhancement_The_Quality_Colloquium _Boston_MA_powerpoint_ppt_presentation

Martin, G., Weaver, S., Currie, G., Finn, R., & McDonald, R. (2012). Innovation sustainability in challenging health-care contexts: embedding clinically led change in rou tine practice. *Health Services Management Research*, 25(190–199). Retrieved from http://www.ncbi.nlm.nih.gov/pmc/articles/PMC366769 3/pdf/10.1177_095148481 2474246.pd

Massachusetts Institute of Technology. (2014). Computer

System Engineering. Retrieved fromThe MIT OCW

website: http://ocw.mit.edu/courses/electrical-

engineering-and-computer-science/6-033-computer-

system-engineering-spring-2009/

McConnell, C. R. (2011). *The Effective Healthcare Supervi*

sor. (7 ed.). Jones and Bartlett.

McClellan, S., Casalino, L., Shortell, S., & Rittenhouse

(2013). When does adoption of health information

technology by physician practices lead to use by phy

sicians within the practice? *J Am Med Inform Assoc,*

20(e1), e26–e32. Retrieved from

http://www.ncbi.nlm.nih.gov/pmc/articles/PMC371533

6/pdf/amiajnl-2012-001271.pdf

McLaughlin, K. (2005). ITIL catches on. *Computerworld,*

3(44), 39-42. Retrieved from

http://academicguides.waldenu.edu/hinf6130

McFadden, K. L., Stock, G. N., & Gowen, C. R. (2006, April

4). Exploring strategies for reducing hospital errors.

Journal of Healthcare Management, 51(2), 123–135.

Retrieved from

http://www.redorbit.com/news/health/456315/explorin

g_strategies_for_reducing_hospital_errors/

McKinney, M. (2007). HIPAA and HITECH: Tighter control

of patient data. *Hospitals and Health Networks, 83*(6),

50-52. Retrieved from

http://academicguides.waldenu.edu/mmha6265

McMillan, D. (2014, December 27). Competencies. (A. Wyatt,

Interviewer). DM@CDentac.com: Carolina Dentac

McNeill, L., Puleo, E., Bennett, G., & Emmons, K. (2007).

Exploring social contextual correlates of computer

ownership and frequency of use among urban, low-

income, public housing adult residents. *J Med Internet

Res, 9*(4). Retrieved from

http://www.jmir.org/2007/4/e35/

Menachemi, N., Saunders, C., Chukmaitov, A., Matthews, M.

C., & Brooks, R. G. (2007). Hospital adoption of in

formation technologies and improved patient safety: A

study of 98 hospitals in Florida. *Journal of Healthcare

Management, 52*(6), 398–410. Retrieved from

http://www.ncbi.nlm.nih.gov/pubmed/18087980

Mensah, E. (2012). Editorial, *Online Journal of Public Health

Informatics, Vol, 4*(3) Retrieved from

http://www.ncbi.nlm.nih.gov/pmc/articles/PMC361583

4/pdf/ojphi-04-19.pdf

Meredith, J.R., Shafer, S.M., Mantel, S.J. & Sutton, M.M.

(2014). *Project management in practice* (5th ed.). Hobo

ken, NJ: John Wiley & Sons, Inc.

MicrosoftHealVault. (2014). Overview. Retrieved from

https://www.healthvault.com/us/en/overview

Miller, S. B. (n.d.). Educational framing. (A. Wyatt,

Interviewer). DC Department of Behavioral Health, 64

New York Ave., NE, Washington, DC 20002

Steven.miller@dc.gov

Mokhatar, G. (1981). Ancient civilizations of Africa. Berke

ley, CA: UNESCO University of California Press. Re

trieved from

https://books.google.com/books?id=B3LNzqo5i0IC&p

g=PA35&lpg=PA35&dq=diop+%22in+practice+it+is+

possile+to+determine+directly+the+skin+colour+and+

hence+the+ethnic+affiliations+of+the+ancient+Egypti

ans+by+microscopic+analysis+in+the+laboratory;+I+d

oubt+if+the+sagacity+of+the+researchers+who+have+

stud

ied+the+question+has+overlooked+the+possibility.

%22+diop&source=bl&ots=ITCDEJBUIK&sig=O3_F

xgwCNY8RnmemDAVNVnZ0aeI&hl=en&sa=X&ei=

EuirVJrbMsbksATgtID4AQ&ved=0CCwQ6AEwAg#

v=onepage&q&f=false

Monegain, B. (2007, June 25). Partners get serious about

SOA. *Healthcare IT News*. Retrieved from

http://www.healthcareitnews.com/news/partners-gets-

serious-about-soa

Montague, E., & Perchonok, J. (2012). Health and wellness technology use by historically underserved health con sumers: Systemic Review. *J Med Internet Res,14*(3). Retrieved from http://www.ncbi.nlm.nih.gov/pmc/articles/PMC379960 8/?report=classic

Morancea, O., & Costin, H. (2008). View over Appling Informatics Systems in forensic expertise, 1st WSEAS International Conference on BIOMEDICAL ELECTRONICS and BOMEDICAL INFORMATICS (BEBI '08) Retrieved from http://www.wseas.us/e-library/conferences/2008/rhodes/bebi/bebi27.pdf

Moskowitz,D., Guthrie, B., & Bindman, A. (2012). The Role of Data in Health Care Disparities in Medicaid Man aged Care. Medicare & Medicaid Research Review, 2(4). Retrieved from http://www.ncbi.nlm.nih.gov/pmc/articles/PMC400647 5/pdf/mmrr2012-002-04-a02.pdf

Muller, C., Riegle-Crumb, C., Schiller, K., Wilkinson, L., &
Frank, K. (2010). Race and academic achievement in
racially diverse high schools: Opportunity and stratify
cation, *Teach Coll Rec, 112*(4). Retrieved from
http://www.ncbi.nlm.nih.gov/pmc/articles/PMC289334
2/pdf/nihms-179479.pdf

National Academy of Engineering. (2014). Biography: Dr. Irving
P. McPhail. Retrieved from the
NAE.edu website:
https://www.nae.edu/Projects/20762/48130/26774.aspx

National Aeronautics and Space Administration. (2013).
Spinoff: 2013. Retrieved from
http://spinoff.nasa.gov/Spinoff2013/pdf/Spinoff2013.p
df

National Association of State Chief Information Officers.
(2012). The Virginia Corrections Information System
(Virginia Coris). Retrieved from the NASCIO web site
http://www.nascio.org/publications/documents/The-

Virginia-Corrections-Information-System-

(VirginiaCORIS).pdf

National Center for Healthcare Leadership. (2014). NCHL

Health Competency Model. Retrieved from the NCHL

website:

http://www.nchl.org/static.asp?path=2852,3238

National Center for Healthcare Leadership, Institute for Diversity

in Health Management, American Hospital Association,

& American College of Healthcare Executives. (2004).

Strategic leadership: Does your hospital reflect the com

munity is serves? Retrieved from the American Hospital

Association web site:

http://www.aha.org/aha/content/2004/pdf/diversitytool.pd

f

National Center for Health Statistics. (2009). Health, United

States, 1983. HHS publication no. (PHS) 84-1232.

Retrieved from HHS web site:

http://minorityhealth.hhs.gov/assets/pdf/checked/1/AN

DERSON.pdf

National Information Center on Health Services Research and Health Care Technology. (2008). *Behavioral Risk Fac tor Surveillance System.* Retrieved from the National Information Center on Health Services Research and Health Care Technology website: http://www.nlm.nih.gov/nichsr/usestats/behavioral_ris k_factor.html

National Information Center on Health Services Research and Health Care Technology. (2010). *Community Health Status Indicators.* [Transcript] Retrieved from: http://www.nlm.nih.gov/nichsr/healthindicators/Comm unity_Health_Status_Indicators_transcript.html

National Institute of Dental and Craniofacial Research. (2014). Oral Cancer: What African American Men Need to Know. Retrieved from the NIDCR web site:http://www.nidcr.nih.gov/oralhealth/Topics/O ralCancer/AfricanAmericanMen/

Nee, O., Hein, A., Gorath, T., Hülsmann, N., Laleci, G. B., Yuksel, M., Olduz, M., Tasyurt, I., Orhan, U., Dogac, A., Fruntelata, A., Ghiorghe, S., Ludwig, R. (2008, Feb). SAPHIRE:intelligent healthcare monitoring based on semantic interoperability platform: pilot applications, *IET Communications, 2* (2), p192-201. Retrieved from http://ieeexplore.ieee.org/xpl/login.jsp?tp=&arnumber=4479512&url=http%3A%2F%2Fieeexplore.ieee.org%2Fiel5%2F4105970%2F4479509%2F04479512.pdf%3Fisnumber%3D4479509%26arnumber%3D4479512

Needleman, J. (2003). *Assessing the financial health of hospitals.* Retrieved from HHS website: http://archive.ahrq.gov/data/safetynet/needleman.htm

Niazkhani, Z., Pirnejad, H., Berg, M., and Aarts, J. (2009). The impact of computerized provider order entry systems on inpatient clinical workflow: a literature re view. *J Am Med Inform Assoc. 2009 Jul-Aug; 16*(4): 539–549. Retrieved from http://www.ncbi.nlm.nih.gov/pmc/articles/PMC270525 8/

Nugent, M. (2010). Payment reform, accountable care, and risk: Early lessons for providers. *Healthcare Financial Man agement: Journal of the Healthcare Financial Manage ment Association, 64*(10), 38–42. Retrieved from http://www.navigant.com/~/media/WWW/site/download s/healthcare/october%202010%20nugent.ashx

Nunez-Smith, M., Bradley, E., Herrin, J., Santana, C., Curry, L., Normand, S., & Krumholz, H. (2011). Quality of care in U.S. territories. *Arch Intern Med, 171*(17): 1528–1540. Retrieved from http://www.ncbi.nlm.nih.gov/pmc/articles/PMC325192 6/pdf/nihms343073.pdf

Oak Ridge National Laboratory. (2014). Environmental Data Science and Systems. Retrieved from the ORNL web site: http://www.ornl.gov/science-discovery/clean-

energy/research-areas/climate-

environment/environmental-data-science-and-systems

Oberlander, J. (2012). Unfinished journey -- A century of health

care reform in the United States. *The New England*

Journal of Medicine, 367(7), 585-90. Retrieved from

http://www.nejm.org/doi/full/10.1056/NEJMp1202111

Ofili, E., Fair, A., Norris, K., Verbalis, J., Poland, R., Bernard,

G., Stephens, D., Dubinett, S., Imperato-McGinley, J.,

Dottin, R., Pulley, J., West, A., Brown, A., &

Mellman, T. (2014). Models of interinstitutional part

nerships between research intensive universities and

Minority Serving Institutions (MSI) across the Clinical

Translation Science Award (CTSA) Consortium. *Clin*

Trans Sci, 6(6), 435-443. Retrieved from

http://www.ncbi.nlm.nih.gov/pmc/articles/PMC403838

4/pdf/nihms563694.pdf

Ohio State University. (2014). Clinical and Translational

Informatics. Retrieved from the OSU College of Medi

cine website:

http://medicine.osu.edu/bmi/research/clinicaltranslatio

nal/pages/index.aspx

Ohlheiser, A. (2014, December 30). This season's flu activity

has reached the epidemic threshold, the CDC says.

Washington Post. Retrieved from

http://www.washingtonpost.com/news/to-your-

health/wp/2014/12/30/this-seasons-flu-activity-has-

reached-the-epidemic-threshold-the-cdc-says/

Ogbu, J. (2003). Black American students in an affluent

suburb: A study of academic disengagement (sociocul

tural, political, and historical studies in education).

Mahwah, New Jersey: Lawerence Erlbaum Associates,

Inc.

Özdemir, V., Borda-Rodriguez, A., RM, Dove, E., Cornejo-

García JA, Viola M, Barbaud A,Ferguson, L., Huzair,

F., Manolopoulos, V., Masellis, M., Milius, Djims, M.,

Warnich, L., & Srivastava, S. (2013). Public health pharmacogenomics and the design principles for global public goods-moving genomics to responsible innova tion. *Current Pharmaceutical and Personalized Medi cine, 11*(1), 1-4 2770–2777. Retrieved from http://www.benthamscience.com/cppm/

Panahi, M., Nie, W., & Lin, K. (2010). RT-Llama: Providing Middleware Support for Real-Time SOA. *Internation al Journal of Systems and Service-Oriented Engineer ing (IJSSOE), 1*(1), 62-78. doi:10.4018/ijssoe.2010010104

Panel on Measuring Medical Care Risk in Conjunction with the New Supplemental Income Poverty Measure (2007). Medical care economic risk: Measuring financial vulner ability from spending on medical care. Washington, D.C: National Academies Press. Retrieved from http://www.nap.edu/download.php?record_id=13525

Parente, S. T., & Van Horn, R. L. (2006). Valuing hospital

investment in information technology: Does governance

make a difference? *Health Care Financing Review, 28*(2),

31-43. Retrieved from http://www.cms.gov/Research-

Statistics-Data-and-

Sys

tems/Research/HealthCareFinancingReview/Downloads/

06-07Winpg31.pdf

Patel, N. (2010, June). Integrating three-dimensional digital

technologies for comprehensive implant dentistry.

Journal of the American Dental Association, 141, 20S-

24S. Retrieved from:

http://jada.ada.org/content/141/suppl_2/20S.short

Payne, T. (2000, August). Computer decision support systems.

Chest, 118(2), 47S-52S. Retrieved from

http://journal.publications.chestnet.org/pdfaccess.ashx?

ResourceID=2157418&PDFSource=13

Payne, P., Pressler, T., Sarkar, I., & Lussier, Y. (2011). People,

organizational, and leadership factors impacting informat

ics support for clinical and translational research. *BMC Med Inform Decis Mak,13*(2). Retrieved from http://www.ncbi.nlm.nih.gov/pmc/articles/PMC3577661/ pdf/1472-6947-13-20.pdf

Payne, T., Bates, D., Berner, E., Bernstam, E., Covvey, H.D., Frisse, M., Graf, T., Greenes, R., Hoffer, E., Kuperman, G., Lehmann, H., Liang, L., Middleton, B., Omenn, G., & Ozbolt, J. (2013). Health information technology and economics, *J Am Med Inform Assoc, 20*(2), 212-217. Re trieved from http://www.ncbi.nlm.nih.gov/pmc/articles/PMC3638175/ pdf/amiajnl-2012-000821.pdf

Pevnick, J., Claver, M., Dobalian, A., Asch, S., Stutman, H., Tomines, A., & Fu, P. (2012). Provider stakeholders' perceived benefit from a Nascent Health Information Exchange: A qualitative analysis. *J Med Syst, 36*(2). Retrieved from http://www.ncbi.nlm.nih.gov/pmc/articles/PMC331303

2/pdf/10916_2010_Article_9524.pdf

Pike, H. (2009, April). HIPAA gets new privacy rules. Infor

mation Today, 26(4), 13-15. Retrieved from

http://www.infotoday.com/it/apr09/index.shtml

Poticny, D., & Klin, J. (2010, June). CAD/CAM in office

technology: Innovations after 25 years for predictable,

esthetic outcomes. *Journal of the American Dental As*

sociation, 141, 5S-S. Retrieved from:

http://www.jada-

plus.com/content/141/suppl_2/5S.abstract

Pozgar, G. D. (2013). *Legal and ethical issues for health profess*

sionals (3rd ed.). Burlington, MA: Jones and Bartlett.

Project Management Institute, Inc. (2013). *A guide to the Project*

Management Body of Knowledge(PMBOK® guide) (5th

ed.). Newtown Square, PA: Author.

Pronovost, P., Rosenstein, B., Paine, L., Miller, M., Haller, K.,

Davis, R., Demski, R., & Garret, M. (2008). Paying the

piper: investing in infrastructure for patient safety. *Jt*

Comm J Qual Patient Saf., 34(6), 342-8. Retrieved

http://www.ncbi.nlm.nih.gov/pubmed/18595380

Public Health Informatics Institute. (2014). Home. Retrieved

from http://www.phii.org

Ramly, E., & Flatley Brennan, P. (2012). Guiding the Design

of Evaluations of Innovations in Health Informatics: a

Framework and a Case Study of the SMArt SHARP

Evaluation, AMIA Annu Symp Proc. 1375-1384. Re

trieved from

http://www.ncbi.nlm.nih.gov/pmc/articles/PMC354044

2/pdf/amia_2012_symp_1375.pdf

Richesson, R., & Nadkarni, P. (2011). Data standards for

clinical research data collection forms: current status

and challenges. *J Am Med Inform Assoc. 2011 May-

Jun; 18*(3):341–346. Retrieved from

http://www.ncbi.nlm.nih.gov/pmc/articles/PMC298078

5/

Richardson, J., Abramson, E., Pfoh, E., Kaushal, R., and the

HITEC Investigators. (2011). How communities are lev
eraging the health information technology workforce to
implement electronic health records. *AMIA Annu Symp
Proc,* 1186-1195. Retrieved from
http://www.ncbi.nlm.nih.gov/pmc/articles/PMC3243241/
pdf/1186_amia_2011_proc.pdf

Riley, J. L. (2014-06-17). Please Stop Helping Us: How
Liberals Make It Harder for Blacks to Succeed. En
counter Books. Kindle Edition.

Ronaldson K., & McNeil J. (2009). Improving drug safety by
locating genetic markers for hypersensitivity reactions.
Medical Journal of Australia, 190(11), 641–643. Re
trieved from
http://www.ncbi.nlm.nih.gov/pubmed/19485844

Rowe, K., & Moodley, K. (2013, March 21). Patients as
consumers of health care in South Africa: the ethical
and legal implycations, *BMC Med Ethics.* Retrieved
from

http://www.ncbi.nlm.nih.gov/pmc/articles/PMC361487
2/pdf/1472-6939-14-15.pdf

Schaetti, C., Ali, S., Chaignat, C., Khatib, A., Hutubessy, R., & Weiss. (2012). Improving community coverage of oral cholera mass vaccination campaigns: Lessons learned in Zanzibar. *PLoS One, 7*(7). Retrieved from http://www.ncbi.nlm.nih.gov/pmc/articles/PMC340240 3/pdf/pone.0041527.pdf

Schmaltz, S., Williams, S., Chassin, M., Loeb, J., & Wachter, R. (2011). Hospital performance trends on national quality measures and the association with Joint Com mission accreditation. *Journal of Hospital Medicine, 6*(8): 454–461. Retrieved from http://www.ncbi.nlm.nih.gov/pmc/articles/PMC326571 4/pdf/jhm0006-0454.pdf

Schiff, G., & Bates, D. (2000, June). Electronic point-of-care prescribing: Writing the 'Script'. *Disease Management & Health Outcomes, 7*(6), 297-304. Retrieved from http://www.questionpoint.org/crs/servlet/org.oclc.ask.

AskPatronFetchQA?&language=1&qid=187715

Schulz, E., Barrett, J., Price, C. (1998). Read code quality

assurance: From simple syntax to semantic stability, *J

Am Med Inform Assoc, 5*(4), 337-346. Retrieved from

http://www.ncbi.nlm.nih.gov/pmc/articles/PMC61311/

pdf/0050337.pdf

Schwartz, N., and Cooper, M. (2013). Racial diversity efforts

ebb for elite careers, analysis finds. NY Times. Re

trieved from

http://www.nytimes.com/2013/05/28/us/texas-firm-

highlights-struggle-for-black-

professionals.html?pagewanted=all&_r=1&

Sellers R., Smith, M., Shelton, J., Rowley, S., and Chavous, T.

(1998). Multidimensional inventory of Black identity:

A reconceptualization of African American racial iden

tity, Personality and Social Psychology Review, 2, 18-

39. Retrieved from

http://www.sagepub.com/thomas2e/study/articles/secti on2/Article37.pdf

Sittig, D., and Singh, H. (2012). Electronic health records and national patient-safety goals. *N Engl J Med. 2012 November 8; 367(19): 1854–1860.* Retrieved from http://www.ncbi.nlm.nih.gov/pmc/articles/PMC369000 3/

Slaughter, A., & Evans, L. (2007). Culturally sensitive oral health educational materials for older African Americans. *Journal of Health Care for the Poor and Underserved, 18.* 868–886. Retrieved from http://www.healthdiversity.pitt.edu/diversity/document s/OralHealthinOlderAfricanAmericans.pdf

Stanford Medicine. (2014). Stanford Center for Medical Informatics. Retrieved from the Standford Medicine website: https://med.stanford.edu/clinicalinformatics.html

Stewart, B., Fernandes, S., Rodriguez-Huertas, E., Landzberg,

M. (2020, March). A preliminarylook at duplicate test

ing associated with lack of electronic health record in

teroperability for transferred patients, *Journal of Amer

ican Informatics Association, 17,* 341-344.doi:

10.1136/jamia.2009.001750

Studer, Q. (2008). *Results that last: Hardwiring behaviors that

will take your company to the top.* Hoboken, NJ:

Wiley.

Subramanian, S., Tangka, F., Sabatino, S., Howard, D.,

Richardson, L., Haber, S., Halpern, M., & Hoover, S.

(2012). Impact of chronic conditions on the cost of

cancer care for medicaid beneficiaries. *Medicare &

Medical & Research Review, Vol 2*(4), E1-E-20, Re

trieved from

http://dx.doi.org/10.5600/mmrr.002.04.a07

Sussman, J. H., Grube, M. E., & Samaris, D. (2009). Ensuring

affordability of your hospital's strategies. *Healthcare Fi

nancial Management, 63*(5), 42-50. Retrieved from

Afroinformatics™

http://www.ncbi.nlm.nih.gov/pubmed/19445399

Tan, L. (2008, February). Surgery with robots: Doctors may soon perform surgery without physically touching the patient, and medical students learn anatomy using vir tual simulators. *Innovation, 8*(1), 65-67. Retrieved from http://academicguides.waldenu.edu/nsei6600

Tan, J. K. H., & Payton, F. C. (2010). *Adaptive health man agement information systems:Concepts, cases, and practical applications.* Sudbury, MA: Jones and Bart lett.

Taylor, V., Erwin, K., Ghose, M., & Perry-Thornton, E. (2001). Models to increase enrollment of minority fe males in science-based careers. *Journal of the National Medical Association, 93*(2): 74-77. Retrieved from http://www.researchgate.net/publication/10842284_M odels_to_increase_enrollment_of_minority_females_in _science-based_careers

Thomas, R., Wilson, D., Justice, C., Birch, S., & Sheps, S.

(2008). A literature review of preferences for end-of-life

care in developed countries by individuals with different

cultural affiliations and ethnicity. *Journal of Hospice*

and Palliative Nursing,10(3), 142–161. Retrieved from

http://www.nursingcenter.com/lnc/pdf?AID=794261&an

=00129191-200805000-

00012&Journal_ID=260877&Issue_ID=794241

Top Coder. (2012). Press Release. Retrieved from the

SpaceRef Interactive, Inc. website:

http://spaceref.com/news/viewpr.html?pid=36738

Tosic, V (2010). Automonic business-driven dynamic adapta

tion of service-oriented systems and the WS-

Policy4MASC support for such adaptation. *Interna*

tional Journal of Systems and Service Oriented Engi

neering 1(1), 79-95. doi: 10.4018/jssoe.2010092105

University of Minnesota. (2014). School of Public Health.

Retrieved from the UM School of Public Health web

site:

Afroinformatics™

http://sph.umn.edu/programs/certificate/informatics/

University of North Carolina Wilmington. (2014). Information

Systems and Operations Management. Retrieved from

the UNCW Career Center website:

http://uncw.edu/career/operationsmanagement.html

Uribe, C., Schweikhart, S., Pathak, D., Dow, M., & Marsh, G.

(2002). Perceived barriers to medical-error reporting:

An exploratory investigation. Journal of Healthcare

Management, 47(4), 263-280. Retrieved from

http://www.library.armstrong.edu/eres/docs/eres/MHS

A7750-1_CROSBY/7750_week2_barriers.pdf

U.S. Census Bureau. (2014). Black Population. Retrieved

November 13, 2014 from the U.S. Census Bureau

website:

http://www.census.gov/population/race/data/black.html

U.S. Courts. (2014). History of Brown v. Board of Education.

Retrieved from the U.S. Courts website:

http://www.uscourts.gov/uscourts/educational-

resources/get-involved/federal-court-activities/brown-
board-education-re-enactment.pdf

U.S. Department of Health and Human Services (n.d.).
Hospital process of care measures. Retrieved from the
Medicare.gov website:
http://www.medicare.gov/hospitalcompare/Data/Meas
ures.html

U.S. Department of Health & Human Services. (2003). OCR
Privacy Rule Summary. Retrieved from the HHS web
site:
http://www.hhs.gov/ocr/privacy/hipaa/understanding/s
ummary/privacysummary.pdf

U.S. Department of Health and Human Services. (2009).
Health Information Technology for Economics and
Clinical Health Act. Retrieved from Retrieved from the
HHS website:
http://www.hhs.gov/ocr/privacy/hipaa/understanding/c
overedentities/hitechact.pdf

U.S. Department of Health and Human Services (2013).

Hospital Compare: A quality tool provided by Medi

care. Retrieved November 16, 2013 from the Medi

care.gov website:

http://www.medicare.gov/hospitalcompare/search.html

U.S. Department of Health and Human Services. (2014a).

Health Information Privacy. Retrieved from the HHS

website: http://www.hhs.gov/ocr/privacy/

U.S. Department of Health and Human Services. (2014b).

About ONC. Retrieved from the HealthIT.gov website:

http://www.healthit.gov/newsroom/about-onc

U.S. National Library of Medicine. (2014a). Databases.

Retrieved from NIH/NLM website

http://www.nlm.nih.gov/

U.S. National Library of Medicine. (2014b). Health Econom

ics Information Resources: A Self-Study Course. Re

trieved from the NIH/HLM website:

http://www.nlm.nih.gov/nichsr/edu/healthecon/index.h

tml

U.S. Securities and Exchange Commission. (2014). Begin
ner's Guide to Financial Statements. Retrieved online
from the SEC website:
http://www.sec.gov/investor/pubs/begfinstmtguide.htm

Valla, J., and Williams, W. (2012). Increasing achievement and
higher-education representation of under-represented
groups in science, technology, engineering, and mathe
matics fields: a review of current K-12 intervention pro
grams. *J Women Minor Sci Eng, 18*(1), 21-53. Retrieved
from
http://www.ncbi.nlm.nih.gov/pmc/articles/PMC3430517/
pdf/nihms395608.pdf

Vanden Berghe, E., Appeltans, W., Costello, M., &
Pissierssens, P. (2004). Proceedings of Ocean Biodi
versity Informatics: An international conference on
marine biodiversity data management. Hamburg, Ger
many, 29 November - 1 December, 2004. (IOC Work

shop Report, 202) (VLIZ Special Publication, 37). Re

trieved from

http://www.jodc.go.jp/info/ioc_doc/Workshop/150008

e.pdf

Van Sante, T., & Ermers, J. (2009). TOGAF™ 9 and ITIL®

V3: Two frameworks whitepaper. Getronics Consult

ing. Retrieved from http://www.readbag.com/best-

management-practice-gempdf-white-paper-togaf-9-itil-

v3-sept09

Varkey, P. (2010). *Medical quality management: Theory and*

practice. Sudbury, MA: Jones & Bartlett.

Virginia Department of Health Professions. (2013). Home.

Retrieved from the VDHP website:

http://www.dhp.virginia.gov/

Vicente, M. (2013). Enterprise Architecture and ITIL. Instituto

Superior T_ecnico, Lisboa, Portugal. Retrieved from

https://fenix.tecnico.ulisboa.pt/downloadFile/39514554

8341/resumo.pdf

Virginia State Advisory Committee to the U.S. Commission on
Civil Rights. (1971). George Mason College: For all the
people? Retrieved from
http://ahistoryofmason.gmu.edu/archive/files/7ea9d9c66
0c5ea03ebb233529abdbcde.pdf

Virology. (2014, September 9). An outbreak of enterovirus 68.
Retrieved from the Virology web site:
http://www.virology.ws/2014/09/09/an-outbreak-of-
enterovirus-68/

Vogels, W. (1999). 17th ACM Symposium on Operating Sys
tems Principles (SOSP'99), Operating Systems Review,
34(5), 93-109. Retrieved from
http://dl.acm.org/citation.cfm?id=319158%C3%DC

Wachter, R. (2010). Patient safety at ten: Unmistakable pro
gress, troubling gaps. *Health Affairs, 29*(1), 165–173.
Retrieved from
http://www.ncbi.nlm.nih.gov/pubmed/19952010

Wager, K. A., Lee, F. W., & Glaser, J. (2009). *Health care information systems: A practical approach for health care management* (2nd ed.). San Francisco: Jossey-Bass.

Ward, J. A. (2013, March). The project manager as Houdini—escaping the triple constraint. Retrieved from http://resources.intenseschool.com/the-project-manager-as-houdini-escaping-the-triple-constraint-2/

Weiner, B. (2009). A theory of organizational readiness for change. *Implementation Science, 4*(67) Retrieved from http://www.ncbi.nlm.nih.gov/pmc/articles/PMC277002 4/pdf/1748-5908-4-67.pdf

West, C. (1993). *Race Matters*. New York: Vintage Books.

World Health Organization (n.d.a). WHO statistical information system, WHOSIS. Retrieved March 21, 2013, from the WHO website: http://www.who.int/whosis/en/

World Health Organization. (n.d.b). Ebola virus disease: Fact sheet 103. Retrieved from the WHO web site: http://www.who.int/mediacentre/factsheets/fs103/en/

Wyllie, T. (2004). Back to basics—practical magic for project management success. *CMA Management, 78*(2), 32-35. Retrieved from http://www.highbeam.com/doc/1G1-116222000.html

Yasnoff, W. A., O'Carroll, P. W., Koo, D., Linkins, R. W., & Kilbourne, E. M. (2000, November). Public health in formatics: improving and transforming public health in the information age. *Journal of Public Health Man agement and Practice, 6*(6), 67–75. Retrieved from http://www.researchgate.net/publication/5827019_Publ ic_health_informatics_improving_and_transforming_p ublic_health_in_the_information_age

Zhang, H., & Su Liu, Q. (2004). Sports Informatics: A New Interdiscipline In Sports Science, Athens 2004: Pre-Olympic Congress. Retrieved from http://cev.org.br/biblioteca/sports-informatics-new-interdiscipline-in-sports-science/

Zelman, W. N., McCue, M. J., & Glick, N. D., Thomas, M. S.

(2014). *Financial management of health care organiza tions: An introduction to fundamental tools, concepts, and applications* (4th ed.). San Francisco, CA: Jossey-Bass.

Zheng, T., Mukamel, D., Caprio, T., Cai, S., & Temkin-Greener, H. (2010). Racial disparities in in-hospital death and hospice use among nursing home residents at the end-of-life. Med Care. 2011 November; 49(11): 992–998. Retrieved from http://www.ncbi.nlm.nih.gov/pmc/articles/PMC321576 1/pdf/nihms330267.pdf

Cultural Quote References

(Listed order of appearance within text)

- **Herbie Hancock**

Herbie Hancock. (n.d.). MusicWithEase.com. Retrieved November 14, 2014, from MusicWithEase.com website: http://www.musicwithease.com/herbie-hancock-quotes.html

- **David Sanborn**

  David Sanborn. (n.d.). BrainyQuote.com. Retrieved January 5, 2015, from BrainyQuote.com website: http://www.brainyquote.com/quotes/quotes/d/davidsan bo513696.html

- **Miles Davis**

  Troupe, Q. (1989). Miles: The autobiography. New York, NY: Simon & Schuster.Troupe, Q. (1989). Miles: The autobiography. New York, NY: Simon & Schuster.

- **John Coltrane**

  John Coltrane. (n.d.). izquotes.com. Retrieved November 13, 2014, from izquotes.com website: http://izquotes.com/author/john-coltrane

  John Coltrane. (n.d.). JazzQuotes.com. Retrieved November 13, 2014, from JazzQuotes.com website: http://jazz-quotes.com/artist/john-coltrane/

- **Terrance Blanchard**

  Paradigm Studio. (Producer), & Vogt, P., Hill, K., Rivoira, M. (Director). (2010). *Icons Among Us: jazz in the present tense* [DVD]

  Dahlia, B. (2010). Study and Discussion Guide [pdf]. Icons Among US: jazz in the present tense. Paradigm Studio

- **Wynton Marsalis**

Paradigm Studio. (Producer), & Vogt, P., Hill, K., Rivoira, M. (Director). (2010). *Icons Among Us: jazz in the present tense* [DVD]

Dahlia, B. (2010). Study and Discussion Guide [pdf]. Icons Among US: jazz in the present tense. Paradigm Studio

- **Alain Locke**

  Charles Molesworth (2012-06-11). The Works of Alain Locke (Collected Black Writings) (p. 93). Oxford University Press. Kindle Edition.

- **Billie Holiday**

  Billie Holiday. (n.d.). BrainyQuote.com. Retrieved January 5, 2015, from BrainyQuote.com website: http://www.brainyquote.com/quotes/quotes/b/billieholi 167425.html

- **Wayman Tisdale**

  Carlson, J. (2009). To the end, Wayman Tisdale was an inspiration. NewsOK. Retrieved from http://newsok.com/to-the-end-wayman-tisdale-was-an-inspiration/article/3369924

- **Cheikh Anta Diop**

  Mokhatar, G. (1981). Ancient civilizations of Africa. Berkeley, CA: UNESCO University of California Press. Retrieved from https://books.google.com/books?id=B3LNzqo5i0IC&pg=PA35&lpg=PA35&dq=diop+%22in+practice+it+is+

possible+to+determine+directly+the+skin+colour+and
+hence+the+ethnic+affiliations+of+the+ancient+Egypt
ians+by+microscopic+analysis+in+the+laboratory;+I+
doubt+if+the+sagacity+of+the+researchers+who+have
+studied+the+question+has+overlooked+the+possibilit
y.%22+diop&source=bl&ots=ITCDEJBUIK&sig=O3_
FxgwCNY8RnmemDAVNVnZ0aeI&hl=en&sa=X&ei
=EuirVJrbMsbksATgtID4AQ&ved=0CCwQ6AEwAg
#v=onepage&q&f=false

- **Dizzy Gillespie**

Dizzy Gillespie. (n.d.) Retrieved November 26 from
APassionForJazz.net website:
http://www.apassion4jazz.net/quotes/dizzy-
gillespie.jpg

- **Matthew Shipp**

Paradigm Studio. (Producer), & Vogt, P., Hill, K.,
Rivoira, M. (Director). (2010). *Icons AmongUs: jazz in
the present tense* [DVD]

Dahlia, B. (2010). Study and Discussion Guide [pdf].
Icons Among US: jazz in the present tense. Paradigm
Studio

- **Wayne Shorter**

Paradigm Studio. (Producer), & Vogt, P., Hill, K.,
Rivoira, M. (Director). (2010). *Icons AmongUs: jazz in
the present tense* [DVD]

Dahlia, B. (2010). Study and Discussion Guide [pdf].
Icons Among US: jazz in the present tense. Paradigm
Studio

- **Charles Mingus**

Charles Mingus. (1977). Wikiquote. Retrieved
November 20, 2014, from Wikiquote.com website:
http://en.wikiquote.org/wiki/Charles_Mingus

- **Booker T. Washington**

Washington, Booker T. (2013-06-02). Up from
Slavery: An Autobiography (Annotated) (pp. 89-90).
Seahorse Publishing. Kindle Edition.

- **Ravi Coltrane**

Paradigm Studio. (Producer), & Vogt, P., Hill, K.,
Rivoira, M. (Director). (2010). *Icons Among Us: jazz
in the present tense* [DVD]

Dahlia, B. (2010). Study and Discussion Guide [pdf].
Icons Among US: jazz in the present tense. Paradigm
Studio

- **Stevie Wonder**

Wonder, S. (Composer). (1977). Sir Duke [song]. [S.
Wonder, Performer] Motown.

- **Jason Moran**

Paradigm Studio. (Producer), & Vogt, P., Hill, K., Rivoira, M. (Director). (2010). *Icons Among Us: jazz in the present tense* [DVD]

Dahlia, B. (2010). Study and Discussion Guide [pdf]. Icons Among US: jazz in the present tense. Paradigm Studio

- **Ernest E. Just**

Just, E. E. (1933) Cortical cytoplasm and evolution. *Am. Nat.* 67: 20-29.

- **Courtney Pine**

Paradigm Studio. (Producer), & Vogt, P., Hill, K., Rivoira, M. (Director). (2010). *Icons Among Us: jazz in the present tense* [DVD]

Dahlia, B. (2010). Study and Discussion Guide [pdf]. Icons Among US: jazz in the present tense. Paradigm Studio

- **Carl Brashear**

Carlbrashear.org (2014). Home. Retrieved from CarlBrasher.org website: http://www.carlbrashear.org/

- **Branford Marsalis**

Manson, D. (Producer), & Apted, M. (Director). (1985). *Bring on the Night* [Motion Picture]. Samuel Goldwyn Company.

- **Jae Sinnett**

Sinnett, J. (Composer). (2012). Still Standing [CD].
[Jae Sinnett, Performer] J-Nett Music: BMI

- **James Watkins**

Watkins, J. (2002, March 31). Virginia Tech Class of
1971 Oral History. (T. Kennelly, Interviewer) VA
Tech. Media Building Sound Booth, Blacksburg, VA.
Retrieved from
http://www.specialcollections.lib.vt.edu/archive/blackh
istory/oralhistories/watkins.html

- **Muhammad Ali**

Ali, M. (2004). The Soul of a Butterfly. New York,
NY: Simon & Schuster

- **Frederick Douglass**

Douglass, Frederick (2011-10-13). The Most Complete
Collection of Written Words & Speeches by Frederick
Douglass [Newly Illustrated] (Kindle Locations 3872-
3874). Northpointe Classics. Kindle Edition.

- **Roy Wilkins**

Ivy, J. (May, 1959). Along the N.A.A.C.P. battlefront:
Charlottesville integration. *Crisis, 66* (5). Retrieved
from
http://books.google.com/books?id=k1sEAAAAMBAJ
&pg=PA301&lpg=PA301&dq=%22dr+philip+wyatt%
22+naacp&source=bl&ots=iCyZ-
PT4dn&sig=l_k473kzvD5Z4TBicZ0u3dmt-
74&hl=en&sa=X&ei=TGxzVJT5BtL2yQTWkoL4Dw

&ved=0CCcQ6AEwAw#v=onepage&q=%22dr%20ph
ilip%20wyatt%22%20naacp&f=false

- **George Benson**

Masser, M. and Creed, L. (Composer). (1977). The
Greatest Love of All [song]. [G.Benson, Performer]
Sony/ATV Music Publishing LLC.

- **Harold Marioneaux**

Marioneaux, H. (2005). Medical School Bridge:
Striving For Students' Success. (KYM KLASS special
to Daily Press). Retrieved from
http://articles.dailypress.com/2005-05-
05/news/0505050040_1_professional-schools-dental-
schools-mcat

- **Nikki Giovanni**

Giovanni, N. (1997). Love Poems. New York, NY:
William Morrow & Company, Inc.

- **Hallie Quinn Brown**

McFarlin, Annjenette Sophie (1975) Hallie Quinn
Brown: Black woman elocutionist. Unpublished
Dissertation, Washington State University. Available
on Digital Dissertations database.

- **Grover Washington, Jr.**

Clinton, W. (1999). Statement of death of Grover
Washington, Jr., United States Government Printing
Office. Retrieved from

http://www.gpo.gov/fdsys/pkg/WCPD-1999-12-
27/pdf/WCPD-1999-12-27-Pg2648-2.pdf

- **Adam Clayton Powell**

Adam Clayton Powell, Jr. (n.d.). Best black history quotes:
Adam Clayton Powell, Jr. on ideas. Retrieved November, 13,
2014 from TheRoot.com website:
http://www.theroot.com/articles/history/2013/07/best_black_h
istory_quotes_adam_clayton_powell_jr_on_ideas.html.

End Notes

Index

OCEAN BIODIVERSITY INFORMATICS

Ocean Biodiversity Informatics (OBI) is the use of computer technologies to manage marine biodiversity information through data capture, storage, search, retrieval, visualization, mapping, modeling, analysis and publication. It uses standardized biology and ecology data schema and exchange protocols. Online systems can become interoperable and integrate data from different sources. OBI enables greater access to more data and information faster than ever before, and complements the traditional disciplines of taxonomy, ecology and biogeography. It is urgently needed to help address the global crises in biodiversity loss, i.e. including fisheries; climate change; and altered marine ecosystems (Costello, Vanden Berghe, & Browman, 2006; Ocean Biodiveristy Informatics, 2004).

ENVIRONMENTAL INFORMATICS

Environmental Informatics applies information science to the management of natural resources. It includes aspects of geographic information; mathematical and statistical modeling; remote sensing; database management; knowledge integration; and decision making. Environmental informaticists advance climate and environmental research by developing integrated data products, data delivery systems and data analysis tools. These tools are applied to predict climate change, improve climate model simulations, model biogeochemical cycles and analyze spatiotemporal metadata. Further, they maintain numerous metadata systems that support research at other government agencies and institutions (Oak Ridge National Laboratory, 2014; Virginia Tech College of Natural Resources and Environment, 2014).

Environmental Informatics Careers include:

Environmental data scientists and **eco-informaticists** (Oak Ridge National Laboratory, 2014; Virginia Tech College of Natural Resources and Environment, 2014).

NASA
INFORMATICS

NASA has long used IT and informatics applications towards science, i.e. climate informatics and cloud strategies, and space research explorations. Respecting health contributions, NASA's Jet Propulsion Laboratory Early Detection Research Network (JPL EDRN) Informatics Center develops data-intensive informatics solutions to support the capturing, processing, managing, distributing and analyzing data from cancer biomarker research. The earlier cancer is detected, the more effective the treatment. The JPL EDRN's mission is to research biomarkers, i.e. indicators of disease or the potential for disease (Monteleoni et al. 2013; NASA, 2014; Tiag.net, 2014).

SPORTS
INFORMATICS

Sports Informatics (SI) concentrates on diverse applications of bioinformatics and computer technologies in health, fitness, and sports for solutions on current complex health problems, fitness guidance and sports science developments. It combines sports-related research, education, performance diagnostics and training sciences. SI mainly uses computer technologies and computational biology methods to explore and manage data in health and sports setting. It derives knowledge by mixing, matching, and selecting from bioinformatics, medical informatics, cognitive science, statistics and sports/exercise science. Typical SI systems originate from physiological, psychological, fitness, and specific motor skills profiles of athletes. Based on evidence-based practices, SI systems combine integrated access to individual athletic performance and diagnostics data with EHRs and electronic educational schemes. SI is serviceable to student athletes or professional athletes, coaches, trainers, and therapists. It affords team collaboration through web conferencing, digital media archives and remote conferencing (Institute of Training and Sport Informatics, 2006; Zhang, & Su Liu, 2004).

MEDICAL FORENSIC
INFORMATICS

Forensic Informatics is widely used in medicine and research today to yield forensic DNA analysis. Applications allow forensic specialists to deliver a series of data interpretations with reduced subjectivity. Some applications can simultaneously evaluate approximately one million genetic locations throughout the human genome for more comprehensive results. Forensic Informatics overcomes the challenges of mixed DNA samples aimed at truthful conclusions (Center for Advanced Forensics, 2014; MORANCEA & COSTIN, 2008).

RESEARCH
INFORMATICS

Clinical and Translational Informatics encompasses the biomedical informatics sub-domains of clinical research informatics, translational bioinformatics, imaging informatics, and their intersections with clinical informatics and public health informatics. Careers target the application of informatics theories, methods, and emergent technologies respecting fundamental data, information, and evidence-based management for clinical care and research; imaging and translational research domains (AMIA, 2014; Columbia University, 2014; Ohio State University, 2014).

BioHealth Informatics and BioMedical Informatics

Bio-Health (BHI) and Bio-Medical Informatics (BMI) represent the study of IT in biology and health. Researchers study and manage information respecting behavioral decisions, computational methods, and sharing evidence-based knowledge. These include genome sequencing or variants. BMI couples the biomedical sciences, i.e. biology, medicine, dentistry, nursing, pharmacy, allied health, etc., with information sciences, i.e. computer science, management and decision science, statistics, biostatistics, engineering and information technology, cognitive science, operations research, physics, applied mathematics, etc. Applicable uses include; community, consumer health and social informatics; learning healthcare systems for clinical intelligence, translational biomedical and clinical informatics; big data, data analytics and data science (Columbia University, 2014; Ohio State University, 2014).

Translational Bioinformatics

Translational Bioinformatics is the development of analytical and interpretive methods into evidence-based health practices. It includes research on the integration of biological and clinical data towards the evolution of clinical informatics based on biological observations. Further, it generates insights gained from informatics analysis for diagnoses, prognosis, and therapeutics for improved outcomes. Knowledge derived from transitional bioinformatics may be shared with stakeholders, i.e. biomedical scientists, clinicians, and patients (AMIA, 2014; Harvard Medical School, 2014).

Clinical Research Informatics

Clinical Research Informatics involves the use of informatics in the discovery and management of new knowledge relating to health and disease. It includes management of information related to clinical trials and also involves informatics related to secondary research use of clinical data. Clinical research informatics and translational bioinformatics are the primary domains related to informatics activities to support translational research (AMIA, 2014; Ohio State University, 2014).

Informatics Research Scientist (Computational Materials Science)

A research informatics scientist/engineer functions as a computational expert in materials science. This includes computational prediction and analysis specialization. Their research contributes to leadership on research facility development and in defining both transformational and translational research activities for organizational activities.

HEALTH
INFORMATICS

Primary Care Informatics

Primary Care Informatics involves computer and information technology applications for the practice, research, or teaching of Family Practice, General Internal Medicine, Pediatrics, Advanced Practice Nursing, and Geriatrics. These include clinical workflow, quality assurance, and health outcome improvements. The International Medical Informatics Association has listed *Informatics in Primary Care* as their official journal (AMIA, 2014; International Medical Informatics Association, 2014).

Clinical Informatics

Clinical Informatics is the application of informatics and information technology to deliver health care services. It is also referred to as applied clinical informatics and operational informatics. AMIA considers informatics when used for healthcare delivery to be essentially the same regardless of the health professional group involved, i.e. dentist, pharmacist, physician, nurse, or other health professional. It is concerned with information used in health care by clinicians. Clinical Informatics includes a wide range of topics ranging from clinical decision support to visual images, e.g. radiological, pathological, dermatological, ophthalmological, etc.; from clinical documentation to provider order entry systems; and from system design to system implementation and adoption issues. It includes the use of cohort tools and data review tools for shared evidence-based information (AMIA, 2014; Stanford, 2014).

Clinical Informatics Careers include:

Physician informaticists, clinical informaticists, practitioner consultants, dental informaticists, nurse informaticists, pharmacy or pharmaco-informaticist, and **health informatics technicians** (AMIA, 2014; Bureau of Labor Statistics, 2014; Hebda & Czar, 2013; HIMSS, 2014).

Dental Informatics

Dental Informatics is health informatics with an emphasis on dental treatment. It is a specialization within Health Informatics. Similar to clinical informatics, it uses HIT applications for better dental care, research, and education, i.e. provider and patient (ADA, 2014; AMIA, 2014).

Nursing Informatics

Nursing Informatics is the "science and practice (that) integrates nursing, its information and knowledge, with management of information and communication technologies to promote the health of people, families, and communities worldwide" (IMIA Special Interest Group on Nursing Informatics, 2009). Nurse informaticists work as communication and IT developers, educators, researchers, i.e. chief nursing officers, chief information officers, tele-health home care coordinators, consultants, and policy developers for better healthcare delivery. It integrates nursing science, computer science, and information science to manage and communicate data for evidence-based practices through HIT (AMIA, 2014; HIMSS, 2014).

Pharmacy/Pharmaco-Informatics

Pharmacy and Pharmaco-Informatics are intersections of informatics, HIT, and medication management for patient safety, efficiency, and improved treatment. Pharmaco-informatics is the study and application of more precise drug therapy and regimens for increased safety and effectiveness (Jelliffe, Bayard, Schumitzky, Milman, & Van Guilder, 1994). Both include all aspects of research, analytics, standards development, and clinical practice in the medication use process for prescribing, verifying, dispensing, interpreting, translating and perfecting medication orders. This includes clinical decision support, monitoring, and educating for professionals and patients (AMIA, 2014; Jelliffe, Bayard, Schumitzky, Milman, & Van Guilder, 1994).

Health Informatics Technician

Medical records or health information clerks or technicians organize and manage health information data. They help ensure the quality, accuracy, accessibility, and security respecting EHRs and PHRs. They use various classification systems to code and categorize patient information for insurance reimbursement purposes, databases and registries, and to maintain patients' medical and treatment histories (Bureau of Labor Statistics, 2014; Hebda & Czar, 2013).

Informatics Certifications (from AMIA website):

AMIA offers a Clinical Informatics Board Review Course to provide a comprehensive review of the core content for Clinical Informatics that will be the basis for the examination for certification. The CME eligible course is offered live and online and helps physicians identify those areas where they may need further study. Physicians in all 24 subspecialties are now eligible to become Board Certified in Clinical Informatics through an exam offered by the American Board of Preventive Medicine.

AMIA continues to pursue steps towards developing Advanced Inter-professional Informatics Certification. Recognition of the certification path for board certified physicians is one step forward for the profession. It does not represent the totality of AMIA's certification-related activities. AMIA recognizes that the opportunity for subspecialty certification is relevant to a majority of its members. An equivalent level of certification is being pursued for informaticians who have equivalent competencies (AMIA, 2014).

HEALTH CARE ADMINISTRATION

Health care administration informatics applications support the business side of health care respecting coding, compliance, privacy, billing, and re-imbursement (Hebda & Czar, 2013). Organizations such as the AAPC provide methods for acquiring related certifications for over 20 coding specialties to include professional service coding (CPC®), hospital outpatient (CPC-H®) and hospital inpatient (CIC™) coding, payer perspective coding (CPC-P®), professional billing (CPB™), medical auditing (CPMA™), medical compliance (CPCO™), and physician practice management (CPPM™). Specialty coding credentials are currently offered in more than 20 different fields of expertise (AAPC, 2014; Hebda & Czar, 2013).

Healthcare Administrative Informatics Careers include:

Medical records and coding department supervisors or managers; medical and inpatient coders; coding auditors; release of information specialists; and **consumer health informaticians** (AAPC, 2014; HIPAA Academy, 2014).

Medical and Inpatient Coder

The primary purpose of medical and inpatient coders is to assign ICD-9 and MS DRGs codes according to national and hospital guidelines.

Coding Auditor

The goal of coding auditors is to target and evaluate procedural and diagnosis code selection as determined by physician documentation weaknesses for process improvements (AAPC, 2014).

Release of Information Specialist

A release of information specialist or a Certified Security Compliance Specialist™ (CSCS™) maintains information pertaining to HIPAA/HITECH Privacy training, audits, complaints and resolutions for health organizations. They perform trending, analysis and metric reporting related to privacy breaches and conduct organizational privacy education programs (HIPAA Academy, 2014).

Consumer Health Informatics

Consumer Health Informatics is devoted to consumer or patient feedback. These include patient-centered medicine and health education. Consumer health informatics also targets patient competencies for PHR management and Wellness Informatics.

INFORMATION SYSTEMS ARCHITECTURE & OPERATIONS MANAGEMENT

Information Systems (IS) architects and operations managers (OM) combine quantitative methods and analytical approaches to solving problems in all areas of business utilizing IT and HIT. They apply technology solutions to organizational problems related to the delivery of products and services to the end-user (Arlotto, Birch, Crockett, & Irby, 2007; University of North Carolina Wilmington, 2014).

IS and OM Careers include:

Computer systems engineers, IS quality assurance testers, clinical analysts, sustainability analysts, analytic reporting developers, data analysts, medical informatics researchers, IT clinical analysts, and **implementation project managers** (Arizona State University, 2014; Educational Portal, 2014; Gwinnett Technical College, 2014; Massachusetts Institute of Technology, 2014; PMI, 2014).

Clinical and Sustainability Analyst

Clinical analysts use informatics applications to solve clinical problems. Their roles are to support clinical quality, financial performance, and population health by gathering, analyzing, interpreting and presenting data to the internal and external health organizational stakeholders through consultations for decision making. They provide insightful clinical and financial analyses to the end-users, i.e. clinicians and administrators, for sustainability. They also produce quality assurance reports for safety, satisfaction and better outcomes or exploratory data analyses of reports and datasets, i.e. medical claims and pharmacy data. Clinical and sustainability analysts also identify need changes to workflow procedures and/or system configuration modifications. They are common to hospitals; mental health or nursing care facilities; large medical groups or clinics (Education Portal, 2014; Gwinnett Technical College, 2014).

Computer Systems Engineer

Computer systems engineers often work as part of teams, i.e. providers, researchers, and scientists, within organizations by designing, analyzing, installing, and maintaining information systems in multi-platform and complex environments. They serve as consultants to both internal and external stakeholders. Further, computer systems engineers provide technical support through the allocation of systems resources, management of accounts, password administration, security breach protocols, recoverability and access (Arizona State University, 2014; Massachusetts Institute of Technology, 2014).

IS Quality Assurance Tester

The need for insuring IS quality through quality assurance methods has increased as clinical vocabularies have grown within clinical information systems (Schulz, Barrett, & Price, 1998). QA Testers analyze, design, develop, configure, test, and implement large systems for interoperability and operational sustainability. Essential functions and responsibilities include web, regression, end-user, functional, system, integration, and end-to-end testing through system analysis (University of North Carolina Wilmington, 2014).

Implementation Project Manager

Implementation PMs provide oversight of an informatics system implementation through prioritized leadership to all stakeholders, i.e. CDS teams, physicians, vendors, IT, and organizational administration leaders. They work with implementation support specialists and lead through evidence-based Project Management Principles (Gwinnett, 2014; PMI, 2014).

GLOBAL & PUBLIC HEALTH INFORMATICS

Public health officials use communications science and IT to address the spread of infectious diseases, emerging health threats, and other public health events. The mission of the global health informatics is the international sharing of evidence-based informatics practices, i.e. public health leadership exchanges, in resource-constrained countries. It provides opportunities to increase informatics capacity, facilitates collaboration in investigations of emerging technologies, and prevention through exchanges of experiences and expertise (AMAI, 2014; Columbia University Mailman School of Public Health, 2014; Public Health Informatics Institute [PHII], 2014).

The Global Public Health Informatics Program (GPHIP) was created in 2008 through the Centers for Disease Control and Prevention (CDC) to establish and coordinate CDC's global health informatics initiatives with international partners. It supports country response capabilities and the global strengthening of public health systems through informatics science, principles, strategies and standards (CDC, 2014).

Global and PHI Informatics Careers include:

Public health informaticians, global health informaticians, and **epidemiology informaticists** (AMIA, 2014; Columbia

University Mailman School of Public Health, 2014; PHII, 2014).

Public Health Informatics

Public Health Informatics has been defined as the systematic application of computer science, IT, and HIT to the practice, research, and learning of public health through the collection and analysis of data related to the population health status levels. **It** includes surveillance, prevention, preparedness, and health promotion. Certificates in this field are designed to develop professionals for the systematic application of informatics to public health needs (AMIA, 2014; Johns Hopkins Bloomberg School of Public Health, 2014; PHII, 2014).

Public Health Informatician

Public health informaticians collaborate with other health professionals for better health status levels. They attempt to manage useable data effectively for proper assessments and advocating for needed population health modifications. They work closely with public health policy-makers to present the information required for effective policy development and evaluation. Responsibilities include the ability to conceive, design, develop, implement, and use IT through informatics in the public health domain (AMIA, 2014; PHII, 2014).

Epidemiology Informaticist

Epidemiologist and public health leaders have championed the potential of IT and HIT as tools for safeguarding the health of populations, strengthen public health systems, and research improvements to health promotion and disease prevention programs. Epidemiology informaticists explore how informatics can contribute to programmatic interventions in lifestyle-related epidemics, i.e. obesity and tobacco use, or threat prevention, i.e. bioterrorism and infectious diseases. They generate and disseminate evidence-based data respecting disease, health service utilization, and the effects of medical products through the analysis of health care data. Epidemiology Analytics also collaborate globally with international research communities for best practices through methodological research and standardized analytics tools. They support quantitative benefit-risk analysis, genetic epidemiology, data mining, and the analysis of survey data for key stakeholders (Columbia University Mailman School of Public Health, 2014; PHII, 2014).

About the Author

Dr. Wyatt holds a Doctor of Dental Surgery and a Master of Science in Health Informatics degree. For over 20 years he has delivered care within a wide range of health care settings to include private, military, government, state, academic, and non-profit organizations as a solo-practitioner, officer, employee, and volunteer provider. His perspectives respecting disparity reduction through technology are rooted in the common alternative thinking methods that have challenged our society's culture for networked communication. It is his belief that the meaningful use of evolving technology will continue to broaden the appeal and field of career alternatives for minorities into health care and other professional disciplines as vested community stakeholders.

www.ingramcontent.com/pod-product-compliance
Lightning Source LLC
Chambersburg PA
CBHW070933050326
40689CB00014B/3191